D1584165

# BUSINESS
# STUDIES
## BASIC FACTS

HarperCollins*Publishers*

HarperCollins*Publishers*
Westerhill Road, Bishopbriggs, Glasgow  G64 2QT

First published 1990
Fifth edition 2002

Reprint 10 9 8 7 6 5 4 3 2 1 0

© HarperCollins*Publishers* 2002

ISBN 0 00 712180 6

Designed and typeset by Book Creation Services
Limited

Printed in Italy by Amadeus S.p.A.

# Introduction

*Collins Gem Business Studies* is one of a series of illustrated dictionaries of the key terms and concepts used in the most important school subjects. For this edition the text has been updated and colour is now used throughout the book. With its alphabetical arrangement, the book is designed for quick reference to explain the meaning of words used in the subject and so provides a companion both to course work and during revision.

**Bold** words in an entry identify key terms which are explained in greater detail in entries of their own; important terms that do not have separate entries are shown in *italic* and are explained in the entry in which they occur.

Other titles in the *Basic Facts* series include:
Gem *Biology*
Gem *Chemistry*
Gem *Computers*
Gem *Geography*
Gem *Mathematics*
Gem *Modern History*
Gem *Physics*
Gem *Science*
Gem *Technology*

# A

**above the line**   Methods of promotion which allow a firm to reach a wide audience easily. These include methods over which the business has no direct control, such as advertising on television, in newspapers and magazines. Most advertising is above the line in contrast to below the line, which includes methods over which a business has direct control, for example sales promotion, direct mailing, exhibitions, trade fairs and packaging.

**ACAS (Advisory, Conciliation and Arbitration Service)**   An independent body established in 1974 under the Employment Protection Act, whose aim is to help employers and employees resolve trade disputes and improve **industrial relations**. ACAS contains representatives from both the **Confederation of British Industry (CBI)** and the **Trades Union Congress (TUC)**, as well as independent experts on industrial relations. In conciliation, ACAS tries to bring the two sides of a dispute closer together to help them reach an agreement; in arbitration, ACAS will come to a decision about a dispute on behalf of both sides. Most of ACAS's work involves disputes between individuals and their employees, especially over **unfair dismissal**. But ACAS has also been called in to help with large-scale disputes between national trade unions and employers, either to bring the two sides closer together or to reach an independent agreement. ACAS also advises employers and workers on issues such as payment systems, equal pay and conditions of employment.

**accounts**   The financial records of a business that are used by managers, owners, employees, creditors and others to show how well the business is doing. UK businesses are required by the **Companies Act** to disclose financial information to outside parties for tax purposes at least once a year. These annual accounts consist of a **balance sheet** and a **profit-and-loss account**. They are a summary of all the transactions that have been carried out by the business during the financial year. Larger organizations might also produce management accounts, such as **budgets** and forecasts which are for their own internal use.

**accounting ratios**   A way of analysing the performance of a company by comparing key items from the **balance sheet** and **profit-and-loss account**. The comparison is done by using ratios. These are used to show performance in four broad areas – profitability, **productivity**, **liquidity** and **investment**.

(a) *Profitability ratios* show how well the business is doing in terms of its trading performance. Three important profitability ratios are as follows:

(i) Return on Capital Employed (ROCE). Since Capital Employed is always equal to Net Assets, this ratio is also known as the Return on Net Assets.

$$\frac{\text{Net Profit}}{\text{Capital Employed (or Net Assets)}} \times 100$$

This measures how well the business is using its capital to generate profits and is expressed as a percentage. A high percentage indicates a good return on capital employed.

(ii) Mark-up ratio %:

$$\frac{\text{Gross Profit}}{\text{Cost of Goods Sold}} \times 100$$

This ratio shows the amount of profit (as a percentage) added on to the cost price of the goods sold.

$$\frac{\text{Net Profit}}{\text{Capital Employed (or Net Assets)}} \times 100$$

This measures how much Gross or Net profit the business makes for every £100's worth of sales.

(b) *Productivity ratios* show how efficiently a firm is using its assets.

$$\text{Asset Turnover Ratio} = \frac{\text{Sales}}{\text{Capital Employed (or Net Assets)}}$$

This measures the productive use of the assets of a business. It shows the number of times the value of the assets has been covered by sales. A high ratio indicates efficient use of assets.

(c) *Liquidity ratios* show how well a business is able to pay back its short-term debts. Two important liquidity ratios are:

$$\text{(i) Current Ratio} = \frac{\text{Current Assets}}{\text{Current Liabilities}}$$

$$\text{(ii) Acid-Test Ratio} = \frac{\text{Liquid Assets (Current Assets – Stocks)}}{\text{Current Liabilities}}$$

The second is a tighter measure of liquidity because it omits stocks from the **current assets** on the grounds that these might not be easy to turn into cash. **Creditors** will be concerned to see that both ratios remain greater than one to show that the business can cover its current debts. (d) *Investment ratios* show how well a business is performing on behalf of its owners, the **shareholders**, and how good an investment the business might be for outsiders.

$$\text{(i) Return on Equity Ratio (\%)} = \frac{\text{Net Profit after tax}}{\text{Shareholder's Funds}} \times 100$$

$$\text{(ii) Gearing Ratio (\%)} = \frac{\text{Long Term Liabilities}}{\text{Capital Employed (or Net Assets)}} \times 100$$

The first ratio will show shareholders how a business has made use of the capital invested in it. The second shows how much the firm has borrowed compared to the amount of capital provided by shareholders. High levels of borrowing increase the level of risk at which the business is running.

**advertising**    The process of informing a customer about a product or service, and persuading that customer to buy it (sometimes called **above-the-line** sales promotion).  Advertising is designed to create an awareness of the product (informative advertising), and encourage interest in the product (persuasive advertising), in order to improve its sales potential. This can then be converted into actual sales by the other elements of the **marketing mix**, e.g. **distribution**.

Advertising involves communicating with customers through pictures, words, speech and music on a national, regional or local basis through **advertising media**. It is difficult for businesses to know by how much sales are increased by advertising; decisions about how much to spend will depend upon the size of the business, the type of product, the activities of competitors and the overall **marketing** budget. *See also* **merchandising**.

**advertising agency**    An organization that creates **advertising** material on behalf of its clients. Agencies will take the advertising requirements of a business and organize the production of their campaign by designing and producing advertisements and booking space in the **advertising media**. In recent years they have grown in size and importance as expenditure on advertising by business has increased and as a wider range of organizations have used advertising.

**advertising media**    The channels through which businesses and other organizations communicate with their customers. The media available include:

**Television**

– ITV, C4, C5, Satellite, Cable

**Cinema and video**

**Radio**

– Local Commercial Radio

**Newspapers**

– National Daily and Sunday, Regional Daily, Evening and Weekly, Local, Free

**Magazines**

– Weekly, Monthly, Special Interest, Trade, Professional

**Others**

– Posters, Billboards, Vehicles, Packaging, Labels, etc.
– Direct Mail, Catalogues, Internet.

The choice of media appropriate for a business will depend upon the resources available to the business, the **market segment** being aimed at, the geographical location of the customers, the nature of the product and the particular qualities that the media can offer. A marketing campaign will often involve the use of advertising in various media. For example, the banks advertise student accounts on television, in cinemas, in magazines, in newspapers and on posters at the beginning of each college year. Organizations with more limited resources tend to put all their advertising in one sector, for example a restaurant advertising in the local free newspaper.

**Advertising Standards Authority (ASA)**    A voluntary, self-regulatory body set up by the UK **advertising** industry to consider complaints made by customers about non-broadcast advertisements and sales promotions. (Television advertising is regulated by the Independent Television Commission, radio advertising by the Radio Authority.) It expects an advertisement to be legal, decent, honest and true. It discourages newspapers and other media from carrying advertisements that consumers have objected to, and which are found to break the British Code of Advertising Practice. The offending advertiser is also likely to receive adverse publicity.

**after sales service**    The aspects of selling which are aimed at improving the reputation of the business. They include guarantees, warranties, maintenance and repair services, helplines and returns policies such as 'money back if not satisfied'. These services will promote customer confidence and encourage them to buy goods now and in the future.

**agenda** A list of items to be discussed during a meeting. The agenda is sent to each committee member before the meeting.

**amalgamation** The process of joining together, as when one company merges with another, or the joining together of two or more departments in an organization when it is felt that efficiency would be gained with one larger department rather than several smaller ones. During the 1980s many smaller **trade unions** amalgamated into larger groups that had a larger membership and therefore greater bargaining power.

**annual bonus** A fixed amount in addition to basic wages which employees receive once a year, often at Christmas. This **bonus payment** motivates employees and encourages loyalty to the business.

**annual general meeting (AGM)** The statutory meeting of the directors and **shareholders** of a company held once every fiscal year. The shareholders are asked to vote on various proposals the **board of directors** is making about the company, but can also ask the directors questions about the business. At the AGM, the shareholders are also asked to elect members to the board of directors.

**annual percentage rate (APR)**   The true **interest rate** that a customer pays when borrowing money from a financial organization or when buying on credit. Under the **Consumer Credit Act (1974)** a consumer must be told the true cost of what they are borrowing before they take out a loan or sign a credit agreement as it allows borrowers to compare different loans on offer.

**annual report**   A report (legislated for in the **Companies Act** of 1985) issued by a **limited company**, which contains written and financial statements about the progress of the company in the previous financial year. This is to ensure that the **shareholders** receive some information about the business on an annual basis. Nowadays, larger companies produce quite extensive and glossy reports which contain both the basic accounts and also information about the various activities of the company presented in an informative and attractive way. Such a report acts as good **public relations** for the company.

**apprenticeship**   A system whereby young people receive **on-the-job training** through working alongside a skilled worker. In 1993, the government launched a *Modern Apprenticeship* scheme which helps employers provide training for young people. The Modern Apprenticeship scheme leads to a **National Vocational Qualification (NVQ)** of at least level 3.

**appropriation account**   The final part of the trading and **profit-and-loss account** of a business. It shows what the business has done with any **net profit** that it has made. Part of the net profit will be paid as **dividends** to the owners and part will be retained by the company to plough back to finance the growth of the business.

**arbitration**   *See* **ACAS**.

**Articles of Association**   One of the legal documents that the **Registrar of Companies** requires for the setting up of a limited company. It contains the day-to-day rules about how the company will operate and how the **shareholders** will be involved in the business. It is sent to the Registrar of Companies along with the **Memorandum of Association**.

**assets**   What a company owns as represented in the **balance sheet** of a company. **Fixed assets** are long-term assets which are for use in the business and not for re-sale; **current assets** are used in the course of business and will be converted into cash within the next twelve months. The purchase of assets is the use to which a company puts the funds it has raised from its owners and from other sources such as creditors and banks. The assets help generate the income of the company. *Compare* **liabilities**.

**Assisted Areas** Specific geographical areas of the UK which are eligible to receive financial assistance. The government has identified these areas by above average unemployment rates caused by the decline of traditional industries such as coal, shipbuilding and steel, and by below-average Gross Domestic Product. There are two types of Assisted Areas: **Development Areas** and **Intermediate Areas**. These areas could receive *regional selective assistance (RSA)*, grants given to projects which will create or safeguard jobs and pay their own way. *Regional Enterprise Grants (REG)* are available to encourage development in small and medium-sized firms. Firms can gain information about this assistance through the government's **Business Link** network. Assisted Areas also qualify for additional financial help from the European Regional Development Fund (ERDF).

**auditor** An accountant, independent of a company, who is appointed by the **shareholders** to ensure that the annual **accounts** give a true and fair view of the state of affairs of the company, and comply with the **Companies Act**. The accounts should be prepared using the accepted methods of accountancy. Auditors will also try to ensure that the organization's accounting systems do not allow any fraud or stealing to occur from the company's funds. Large organizations might also carry out internal audits themselves to ensure that their accounting practices and procedures are accurate and efficient. *See also* **environmental audit**.

**authorized share capital**  This is the amount of capital that a limited company is allowed to raise from its **shareholders** as stated in its **Memorandum of Association** when it is registered as a company. The amount that it actually raises is its issued **share capital**; a business may not raise its full amount immediately in order to allow for later expansion when a further share issue would be a useful source of finance.

**autocratic leadership**  A style of **leadership** where the power for making decisions, for controlling what happens and for rewarding and punishing the group is all in the hands of the leader. Supporters of this style say that it will lead to greater efficiency and productivity in a group, and that people like to be directed and told what to do. Opponents say that it discourages initiative, causes dissatisfaction and conflict in the group and increases the number of complaints. Whether such a style is successful depends upon the needs of the situation or the task that the group is facing. *Compare* **democratic leadership**.

**average cost or unit cost**  The total **costs** of producing a product divided by the number of units produced. If the total cost of producing chocolate bars

in a factory is £250,000 a week and the output is
1 million bars a week, then the average cost of
producing one chocolate bar is:

$$\frac{£250,000}{1,000,000} \quad = \quad £0.25p$$

Over a short period of time it is expected that, as
output increases, average costs will fall and then rise
again as a factory moves towards its full capacity.
Over a longer period of time, because of **economies
of scale**, a business should experience falling average
costs as it expands in size. But again, it might reach a
point where average costs do start to rise again as
**diseconomies of scale** set in.

# B

**bad debt**   Money which is due but which cannot be collected. When a business offers a customer **credit** for the purchase of a **good** or **service**, then that customer becomes a **debtor** of that business. If that customer is unable, or refuses, to pay back the debt, then it becomes a bad debt for the business, i.e. one that they are unlikely to recover. The business will write off this bad debt by reducing the amount of profit on its **profit-and-loss account** and reducing the number of debtors on its **balance sheet.** Businesses which deal with many small customers, such as a sweet manufacturer selling to many small sweet shops, will expect a certain level of bad debts each year but will try to keep this level to a minimum by careful credit control.

**balance of payments**   A record of the overall results of a country's trading activity with the rest of the world. It includes **imports** and **exports** of goods and services and capital flows into and out of the UK. The government will use the monthly balance of payments figures as an indicator of how well the economy is performing. A deficit on the balance is when the value of imports exceeds the value of exports. A surplus is when the value of exports exceeds the value of imports. A deficit is likely to lead to a fall in the value of a currency against other currencies, which reduces export prices and increases import prices; a surplus will lead to a rise in the value of the currency, which increases export prices and reduces import prices. Thus any business engaged in trade with or competing against overseas companies will be affected by the state of the balance of payments.

**balance sheet**    A statement listing the accounts of a business which shows, at one particular date, what the business owns – its **assets** – and what the business owes – its **liabilities**. The balance sheet always balances because the purchase of its assets must be financed

| Balance Sheet of a Trader as at 30.09.02 | | |
|---|---:|---:|
| | £ | £ |
| Fixed Assets | | 40,000 |
| + Current Assets | 20,000 | |
| – Current Liabilities | 10,000 | |
| = Net Current Assets (Working Capital) | | 10,000 |
| Net Assets (Capital Employed) | | 50,000 |
| Financed by: | | |
| Long-term Liabilities | | 30,000 |
| Capital and Reserves | | 20,000 |
| | | 50,000 |

from either money raised from its owners (**capital**) or from money raised outside the business. It is now usual for a balance sheet to be laid out in the form of a column (*see table*).

**Bank of England** The central bank of the UK, the Bank of England is controlled by the Treasury, although it has the power to change interest rates independently. It is a **public corporation** and acts on behalf of the government to implement **monetary policy** by controlling the **money supply.** It can do this by limiting the amount of money the **commercial banks** can lend. The Bank of England also controls the UK base rate, which is the guideline for all commercial banks. For example when the base rate rises, commercial banks and building societies usually increase their own **interest rates** in line with the base rate. The Bank of England issues and refunds all government loans; it also issues all coins and banknotes in England and Wales.

**bankruptcy** The condition of being unable to meet the demands of **creditors**. When an individual is unable to pay his/her debts, the creditors will apply to the court for that person to be declared a bankrupt. This might be the case when a **sole trader** or **partnership** cannot meet their debts. The creditors will want the remaining **assets** of the business sold so that all or part of the debts can be paid back. A similar process for a company is called **insolvency**.

**barter**    A simple form of economic transaction where one **good** or **service** is exchanged for another good or service. This might occur in markets where there is no system of money for exchange which can represent the value of the two products. The problem with barter is that there is no agreed standard of value against which to measure goods. Barter is still an important means of transaction today, especially among developing economies. It has also been the basis for some trade between Western nations and Eastern Europe.

**basic pay**    *See* **gross pay**.

**batch production**    A common method of organizing production in a factory that falls between **job production** and **flow production**. In manufacturing companies producing a number of products for which there are regular standard orders, the products can be processed in batches. For example, in a furniture manufacturer, in week 1 the machines might process tables, in week 2 chairs and in week 3 cupboards. It is usual for one order to be completed before the next one is started. In between the products, the machinery might have to be adjusted or cleaned, and the finished products might have to be stored as **stock** as more are produced than demanded in a particular week.

**below the line**    *See* **above the line**.

**benchmark**    Standard against which a business measures itself. By comparing its own operations against another firm's, a business can assess its performance objectively and set effective targets. It is important to select a suitable benchmark against which meaningful comparisons can be made, and to do thorough research to obtain all the relevant data on it.

**board of directors**    Those persons elected by the **shareholders** of a company to control that company and to look after their interests. The board is responsible for the overall policy decisions of the company and for appointing the management team that runs the company on a day-to-day basis. The majority of the board will have management responsibilities in the company, but there might also be nonexecutive directors who do not have any responsibilities. These might be well-known industrialists, financiers or politicians who will improve the reputation of a business. All directors will own shares in the business. *See also* **managing director**.

**bonus payment**    A **payments system** where a payment is made in addition to the basic wage. This is used to provide an incentive for the employees to reach production or sales targets, or to stay loyal to the business. For example, workers in a biscuit factory, paid a **basic pay** of £200 a week, might receive a **productivity bonus** of £10 for every 1,000 biscuits they produce above a certain output. A **sales bonus** could be earned by meeting a certain level of sales. An **annual bonus** payment might also take the form of a fixed sum not tied to any output figure (e.g. a Christmas bonus).

**boycott**    A method of industrial action when workers avoid an aspect of their normal duties by refusing to work with a particular piece of equipment or group of people, or refusing to perform a particular task.

**brand**    A trade name or **trademark** created for a product in order to persuade the customer that this product is different from that of competitors. The brand name can be different from the name of the company, e.g. Nescafé is the brand name, Nestlé is the company. Some companies sell several brands of the same product, to enable a wider range of **market segments** to be targeted. Sometimes a brand name becomes the accepted name of all similar products, e.g. Hoover for vacuum cleaners. A company creates a brand image by **advertising** and **merchandising** so customers develop *brand loyalty,* staying loyal to that particular brand and maintaining the brand's **market share**. In recent years, the own branding of large retailers has reduced the influence of manufacturers' brand names in some consumer sectors.

**break-even**    This is the level of sales/output where

neither a profit nor a loss is being made. It is a simple
model, often represented in the form of a graph, which
can show a business the level of sales/output required if
its total revenue is going to cover its **costs**. Break-even
point is where: Total Revenue (*TR*) = Total Costs (*TC*).
(Total Revenue = Price x Sales/ Output; Total Costs =
**Fixed Costs** + **Variable Costs**).

Above break-even point a **profit** is made, below
break-even point a loss is made. In the diagram overleaf,
the break-even level of sales is 500 units.

Break-even can be found by calculation:

$$\text{Break-even} = \frac{\textbf{Fixed Costs}}{\textbf{Contributions per Unit}}$$

where **Contribution** (per unit) = Selling price –
variable cost.

This model can also be used as a basis for pricing
decisions in a business, e.g. in the diagram on page 22
the business must sell more than 500 units at the
current price to make a profit. The business can alter its
break-even point by raising/lowering its price, or
raising/lowering its costs.

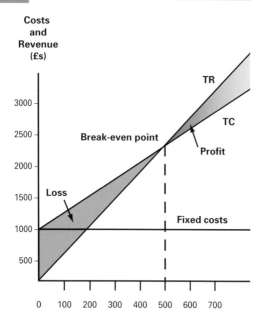

*break-even*

**British Standards Institute (BSI)** A non-profit-making body that establishes the UK standards of safety and quality that consumer products should reach, using its Kitemark as a recognition that the standard has been achieved. The research that the BSI carries out is often used by the British Government when it is trying to improve the safety of consumer goods under the **Consumer Safety Act**. For example, standards exist for prams, cooking utensils, electrical appliances and for toys, which are all now part of the law. Other standards are used voluntarily by the producers, and can act as a guide for consumers that a product is of good quality.

**broker** A person who acts between a buyer and seller in a **market**. Brokers buy and sell in a market not for themselves, but on behalf of others. Common examples are stockbrokers who buy and sell shares on behalf of investors, and insurance brokers who arrange the best insurance for their customers with insurance companies.

**budget** **1.** (of a business) A plan showing the expected **sales revenue** over the coming month or year, matched against the estimated **costs** which will be incurred. Each department is asked to keep to its budgeted costs to ensure that the planned profit is achieved. It is a financial forecast used by a business to plan and control.
**2.** The financial statement that the Chancellor of the Exchequer announces to Parliament each year. The

Budget is a plan of what the Government intends to spend and earn from taxes in the coming year. Any changes to taxation or benefits are announced in the Chancellor's Budget. The Budget also contains a wider report on the state of the British economy.

**building societies**    Institutions that accept savings from investors in return for interest, and lend out money at interest to individuals and firms that are purchasing properties, in the form of **mortgages**. They have usually been non-profitmaking organizations, and have become very successful both in the savings market and in the provision of mortgages. Legislation in the 1980s has allowed building societies to offer a wider range of financial services, and many today operate in a similar way to the **commercial banks**. There has also been a limited move away from the non-profit-making objective; Abbey National was the first to become a **public limited company**, turning its savers into **shareholders**, and more building societies have followed its example. Building societies provide businesses with an important source of long-term finance for the purchase of land, buildings and factory space.

**business activity**    All activities involved in the production of goods and services to satisfy **needs** and **wants**. Business activity refers to any activity related to all business functions, e.g. **production**, **marketing**, **finance** or **personnel department**.

**Business Link**  A government scheme which has set up a network of Business Link companies to provide local businesses with a single point of access to information and support in areas such as marketing and finance. A Business Link company is a partnership between local agencies such as the Chamber of Commerce, **Training and Enterprise Councils** (TECs), Local Authorities and Enterprise Agencies.

**business plan**  A statement prepared by a business to show how it will achieve its aims and objectives. It is used to raise finance to start the business and to monitor the progress the business makes. The plan contains a range of information about the business including details about the original idea, the owners and type of business organization, the location, potential market for the product or service and possible competition, methods of production, costs and pricing strategies, methods of marketing to be used, **cash flow forecast**, methods of finance and future developments.

**business rate**  *See* **Council Tax**.

# C

**CAD**   *See* **computer aided design**.

**CAM**   *See* **computer aided manufacture**.

**capacity**   A general term given for the resources that are available in a business for production, including machinery, plant and labour. The total capacity of a firm determines whether it is able to meet the demand of the customers. If its capacity is insufficient, then customers may go to other producers or become dissatisfied with delays to their order. If it has excess capacity, then resources which are causing **costs** to the business are lying idle. Businesses can increase their capacity in the short run by introducing **overtime** working, by running machines for longer, or by subcontracting work to other producers. In the long run they can expand to larger premises, buy new machinery or take on a larger workforce.

**capital**   **1.** The man-made **factor of production** which refers to all the real **assets** which are used by a business to produce goods and services, such as machinery.
**2.** The money provided by the owner(s) of a business to buy the assets to start production and trading.

**capital goods**  The **stock** of **goods** that exists in a
country which helps in the production of goods and
**services**. Some examples are given below.
*Social capital* or *infrastructure* is provided by the state
for everyone to use to help in production. *Fixed
capital* is not altered by the production process, while
*circulating capital* is transformed or used up by the
production process. The purchase of capital goods by a
business is **investment**.

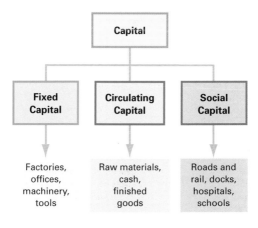

*capital goods*

**capital-intensive**   Relating to a system of production where the production process relies heavily on **capital** as a resource. The number of people employed or the relative cost of labour will be low compared to the amount of capital employed. With more automation of production lines the trend in Western economies has been towards more capital-intensive production methods. Examples of very capital-intensive production are oil refining, chemical production, electricity generation and any major **flow production** system. *Compare* **labour-intensive**.

**cash**   The most liquid of all the **assets** that a business employs, and an important source of **working capital** for a business to help pay wages and bills, and for supplies. Cash includes money in the till, petty cash held in the office and money held in **current accounts** at the bank and in savings accounts which have immediate access. Cash earns no interest so it is important that a business does not hold too much cash; an excess could be used to purchase more productive assets, while too little could lead to **cash flow** problems.

**cash flow**   The flow of money into and out of a business. The diagram, right, shows the major directions of these flows. It is important that a business pays careful attention to its cash flow because if it cannot pay its immediate bills or wages then it will cease operating whatever its level of profitability. A **cash**

*cash flow*

**flow forecast** is a useful tool for a business to see when during the year the business might find itself facing a cash-flow problem. Ways of overcoming such a problem would include increasing sales, reducing costs, arranging further finance through an **overdraft** or **loan**, postponing payment to **creditors**, reducing the level of **debtors** or even selling off some of the **fixed assets** of the business.

**cash flow forecast**    A month-by-month statement which outlines the planned flows of cash into, and out of, a business.

The cash flow forecast indicates when a business will need to raise extra finance. In the example, the business runs short of cash (£400) in August, so it will probably make arrangements for an **overdraft.**

|  | June | July | August |
|---|---|---|---|
|  | £ | £ | £ |
| **Opening cash balance** | 600 | 700 | 600 |
| **+ Cash receipts** | 2000 | 2400 | 1000 |
|  | 2600 | 3100 | 1600 |
| **– Cash payments** | 1900 | 2500 | 2000 |
| **Closing cash balance** | 700 | 600 | (400) |

***cash flow forecast***  *A forecast for 3 months.*

**CBI** *See* **Confederation of British Industry**.

**centralization** A characteristic of an organization with a central body, such as a head office, where all decisions are made. These decisions and policies are then communicated to the branches. **Decentralization** is the situation when the branches of the organization are allowed to make their own decisions.

**certificate of incorporation** A certificate issued by the UK **Registrar of Companies** at the stage of setting up a business when all the other required documents have been drawn up and registered. It shows that the company has its own legal personality separate from its owners. A **private limited company** can now start trading, but a **public limited company** will need to go through the process of offering its shares for sale to the public on the **stock exchange**.

**chain of command** The path in an organization along which decisions or orders will pass from the top of the organization to any particular employee. In a **hierarchy** with a number of levels, the chain of command is likely to be long. In an organization with only a few levels in its hierarchy, the chain of command will be shorter. Too long a chain might mean that decisions take a long time to implement, and that the people at the bottom of the organization do not feel very involved in what is happening. A shorter chain would allow quicker feedback to those in charge and more involvement. (*See* **delegation**.)

**chain of production**     The various stages of production through which a good goes before reaching the consumer. The chain of production shows the links between **primary**, **secondary** and **tertiary production**.

**chairperson or chair**     **1.** The person elected by **shareholders** to be in charge of a **private** or **public limited company** and to represent their interests along with the **board of directors**.
**2.** the person in charge of a meeting who organizes the agenda for the meeting and ensures that the business of the meeting is carried through.

**channel of distribution**     An important element of the **marketing mix** relating to how a business gets its product to the consumer. (*See* **distribution.**) This will involve both the trading route, i.e. the sequence of buying and selling that goes on, and the physical route, i.e. how a product is actually transported or how a service is physically provided. (*See diagram.*) There are three common distribution channels. In A the producer sells direct to the consumer from the factory or through the internet or mail order. This means that the producer does not have to pay any intermediary but will have to bear the costs of storing and distributing the products. In B, the producer sells via a retailer. The producer will allow the retailer to put on a **mark-up** to obtain profit, but the producers will not incur the distribution costs to the consumer. In C, the producer sells via a wholesaler and a retailer. Both will add a margin onto the price of the good but with such a system, a large number of small retailers can be reached. In recent years the importance of the wholesaler and route C has declined, while the use of routes A and B has increased.

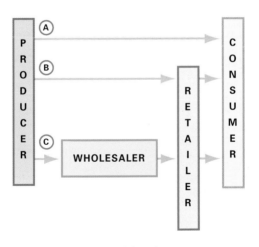

*channel of distribution*

**Choices Training**    A government scheme, managed by **Training and Enterprise Councils (TECs)**, which provides young people with vocational training. This scheme replaces **Youth Training**. The young person will be provided with work experience and some **on-the-job training** in an organization, and some **off-the-job training** in a college. The training can lead to **NVQ** at levels 1, 2 or 3. The trainee receives an allowance during the two years, but there is no guarantee of a full-time post with the organization at the end of two years. From the organization's point of view, the advantages are that it receives a grant from the government covering the cost of some of the trainees, and an opportunity to look at some new recruits before being committed to taking them on full time.

**CIM**    *See* **computer integrated manufacturing**.

**closed shop**    An agreement by which an employee has to belong to a particular **trade union** or group of trade unions in order to work in a certain job. Closed shops are common in craft-based occupations like printing and engineering, and in occupations where labour turnover is high and job security is low, such as the building industry. They exist in order to ensure that those coming into the industry have the correct skills and qualifications, and to give trade unions more bargaining power with management. A closed shop can benefit management because they are negotiating with representatives of the whole workforce in their **collective bargaining**. Under recent employment legislation, the rights of individuals not to be dismissed for not joining a closed shop have been strengthened. A number of **single-union agreements** have been signed between unions and management recently where in return for a closed shop, the union agrees to forego taking **industrial action**.

**cluster sampling**    A method of **sampling** used in **market research** where the population is divided into 'clusters', for example, North-West, North-East. **Random sampling** is then used within the 'cluster'.

**codes of practice**    Voluntary agreements drawn up by a variety of trade associations which aim to make sure that consumers receive a good standard of service in a particular industry. They are not enforced by law, but the trade associations try to make sure that their members keep to the code, and the **Office of Fair Trading** monitors the code for the government. Examples include the code of practice for the motor industry which covers both manufacturers and traders, and the code of practice for the travel industry.

**collective bargaining**    The process whereby representatives of employers and employees (often trade unions) come together to decide upon wages, salaries and other conditions of employment. It occurs at a number of levels, as shown below.

Negotiations at company or industry level tend to be on an annual basis, and cover basic wage rates, conditions of work and redundancy agreements. Negotiations at shopfloor level occur more often and cover local agreements, bonuses and other incentives, recruitment, discipline, and working practices. In both the **public** and **private sectors**, the majority of workers have their pay determined by collective bargaining, although only a minority of managers in the private sector are similarly covered.

| Level | Who is involved? |
|---|---|
| Shopfloor level | Shop Stewards or Union Representatives and Plant Managers |
| Company level | Convenors/Union Officials and Senior Company Managers |
| Industry level | National Union Representatives and National Employers Association |

*collective bargaining*

**commercial bank**    A **public limited company** that
provides **current account** facilities for individuals and
businesses, and takes deposits and provides **loans**.
Banks provide a range of other services for their
customers, and have diversified to offer **mortgages**,
insurance and share dealing. There are four major
commercial banks in England and Wales plus two in
Scotland, with an extensive network of branches
throughout the country. Competition between the banks
has increased in terms of the number of outlets, opening
hours, services offered, accounts for young people, and
the **interest rates** offered on savings accounts. This has
been partly in reaction to increased competition from
savings banks and **building societies**. Banks are an
important source of short-term finance for business
through **overdrafts** and longer-term finance through
**loans**. They also provide information and advice,
especially for small businesses.

**commission**    A type of **piece rate** payment used to
reward sales staff working in shops or travelling
between customers. Payment is based on the number of
sales that are made. For example, in a clothes shop,
sales assistants may receive 1% of the value of what they
have sold in a week as an agreed part of their wage. In
the majority of cases the sales person receives a basic
**wage** based on a **time rate**, and then the commission to
act as an incentive on top of the basic. Commission is
also known as a **sales bonus** and is used for **motivation**.

**commodities**  *See* **goods**.

**common agricultural policy (CAP)**    A policy of the
**European Union** which aims to ensure a common
**market** for all agricultural products between the
member countries of the EU. Agricultural goods can be
traded freely within the EU but a Common External
Tariff against products coming from outside the EU is
imposed. Common prices for products are fixed within
the Community; unfortunately these prices have often
been set too high so that a surplus of goods has been
produced. This has made the policy expensive for
governments as the surplus goods are bought at the
guaranteed price and then put into store. To reduce
surpluses, **quotas** have been introduced to limit the
amount that farmers can produce. The CAP also
provides support for farmers in poorer areas of Europe,
and special concessions are given to agricultural
produce coming from less-developed countries in Asia,
Africa and the West Indies.

**communication**    The sending of messages via a channel
or medium of communication to a target person or group,
and then receiving some feedback from the receiver that
the message has been understood and acted upon. It is a
two-way process between sender and receiver. In
business, communication occurs between **management**,
workforce, customers, suppliers, **creditors**, and so on.
The media used are shown in the diagram.

| **Verbal** | **Visual** |
|---|---|
| Announcements | Posters |
| One-to-one interviews | Graphs and Charts |
| Group meetings | Pictures |
| Company meetings | Video/Films |
| **Written** | **Oral** |
| Memoranda | Telephones |
| Letters | Music |
| Telex/Fax | Radio/Tapes |
| Notices | |
| Electronic mail | |

*communication*

The purpose of communication is to change the behaviour of the receiver. If communication fails, it might be because of a possible barrier to communication arising from the sender, from the medium used, or from the receiver. *See* **written communication**.

**Companies Act**   The name given to legislation that governments pass to regulate the activities of registered companies. Each Companies Act that is passed by

Parliament supersedes the previous act and adds something new to company law. The Companies Act covers the setting up of a company, the raising of capital, the keeping of accounts, the distribution of profits, the way a company is administered, its relationship with **shareholders** and the way it is wound up. Such legislation exists to protect the interests of the **shareholders** and the **creditors**. With membership of the **European Union**, the UK is gradually bringing its own company legislation in line with that of the other member countries so that laws are the same throughout the EU.

**company**   *See* **limited company**.

**competition**   The idea that in a **market** one producer should always be rivalled by another producer to ensure that prices are kept low and the customer is not exploited. This idea is the basic influence in **free-market economies**. Producers can compete using prices, **advertising**, **brand** loyalty, free gifts, etc. Only where a **monopoly** exists, with one dominant producer, is it felt that competition may not exist. Both in the UK and in the US, governments have sought to control monopolies by legislation in order to protect the public interest.

**Competition Act**   An Act passed by the UK Parliament in 1998 which was an extension of the government controls over **monopolies** and **mergers**

contained in the 1973 **Fair Trading Act** and brought UK law in line with EC law. Under this Act, the **Office of Fair Trading** is able to investigate the activities of a person or business that might prove to be anti-competitive. Activities that might be looked into include: price discrimination against certain customers, refusal to supply particular outlets, and unfair price cutting to drive smaller producers in an industry out of business. It also protects against the abuse by one company of a dominant position in the market.

**computer aided design (CAD)**　　Computer programs which enable products to be designed on a computer screen. The design information is stored electronically and this allows the designer to make changes and try out ideas without having to start a new design drawing or build expensive prototypes.

**computer aided manufacturing (CAM)**
Computer programs which allow machines performing tasks to be controlled. These machines can control the temperature of a process, or the rate of flow of a liquid, or they can be programmed to perform tasks requiring a high degree of accuracy.

**computer integrated manufacturing (CIM)**　　This process uses computers to control the whole manufacturing process, from design through to production.

**conciliation**   *See* **ACAS**.

**conditions of service**   The terms on which an employee has been employed by an organization. They are contained in writing in that person's contract of employment. They inform the employee of his or her rights, their rates of pay and method of payment, the hours of work, holiday entitlement, sickness pay, provisions for pension schemes, any disciplinary code and the length of notice required to end the contract. Any changes in these conditions of service would be negotiated between the organization and the employee's representatives.

**Confederation of British Industry (CBI)**   A **pressure group** founded in 1965 to represent major companies, employers' organizations and nationalized industries in discussions with the government and the **Trades Union Congress**. Its aims are to influence industrial, economic and commercial policies in favour of British industry and to develop the effectiveness and efficiency of industry both at home and abroad. The CBI has a membership of some 13,000 organizations as well as a small permanent staff under a Director General. It also has an annual conference. It lobbies local and national government in Britain and also maintains links with the European Commission and other international organizations.

**conglomerate merger**  The joining together in a **merger** of businesses that operate in unrelated areas of activity or at different levels of production. A *conglomerate* is an organization that operates in several unconnected product and market areas. The reasons it does this are to diversify and therefore be able to spread risks if one product or **market** declines. It also allows the company to continue to grow and boosts the performance of its shares. However, such growth may cause problems if the company does not have expertise in the new area. Hanson Trust plc is an example of a conglomerate, owning among other things goldfields, brick producers, tobacco, battery and typewriter companies.

**consultation**  The process whereby **management** discusses with the workforce the decisions and future plans of their organization. This might be done on a regular basis through the meetings of a consultative committee containing representatives of shop floor and management. Unlike **collective bargaining**, consultation does not result in a decision being made; it is the sharing of ideas, plans and concerns. Such consultation is designed to improve **communication** and **motivation** in an organization.

**consumer**  A person who buys **goods** and **services** for his or her own use or consumption. Consumers are recognized as an important group – the government has passed laws to protect them; manufacturers investigate consumer tastes using **market research**.

**Consumer Credit Act (1974)**    A law to protect **consumers** who buy goods on **credit**. The need for such a law came with the growth in the number of consumers buying goods on credit and with more credit facilities available for the public in the form of credit cards, shop cards, loans, hire purchase, etc. The 1974 Act ensures that businesses which lend money are licensed and approved, that the true rate of interest that the consumer is paying (the **annual percentage rate**) is told to the customer, and that normal **consumer protection** applies if goods are faulty. It also states that if people sign a credit agreement at home, then they have a period of up to 12 days to change their mind before it applies to them.

**consumer durable**    A good purchased by a **consumer** that is expected to last for more than one year or be used more than once. Examples include hi-fis, motor cars, refrigerators and sofas. Although still an important element of UK manufacturing output, the number of *imported* consumer durables sold in the UK has increased, especially since the UK joined the **European Union**. Sales of consumer durables have increased with the growth of consumer credit facilities as these goods are often purchased on credit.

**consumer goods**   Products that are purchased by households; they can be classified as either *single-use goods* which are used up as they are consumed, or as **consumer durables** which will last over a period of time.

**consumer panels**   A method of **market research** where a group of **consumers** are surveyed on a regular basis to find out about their buying habits. The group might keep a diary of what they buy to provide more accurate evidence than memory. This type of research is useful for the mass consumer product market and for finding out the likely impact of **advertising** through ascertaining people's reading, watching and listening habits. A problem with this method is that using a sample of consumers as a panel becomes less representative towards the end of the research period as they become too interested in the product; they stop being typical consumers and become experts.

**consumer protection**   Safeguarding the interests of the **consumer**. This was originally left to the buyer – *caveat emptor* (let the buyer beware) – but with the growth in the number of products on offer, and the size of the companies producing and selling them, it has become much more difficult for consumers to protect their own interests. Thus a movement for consumer protection has emerged since the 1960s in both the UK and other developed countries. In the UK, groups like the **Consumers' Association** and the National

Consumer Council have formed to protect the interests of the consumer and legislation like the **Trade Descriptions Act** and the **Fair Trading Act** have been passed where the government have felt it necessary to intervene on behalf of the consumer. The areas where consumer protection has been seen as most important have been the way goods and services have been described, labelled and advertised; the quality and safety of goods; the standards and hygiene of food sales; buying on credit and guarantees.

**Consumer Protection Act (1987)**  A law which was passed to bring consumer protection in the UK into line with EU **legislation**. This law allows consumers to sue a business for any damage caused to them by defective goods. For example, if a defective gas appliance caused damage to a consumer, that person could sue the business for compensation. This Act also protects consumers against misleading prices, especially 'special offers' which are not genuine.

**Consumer Safety Act (1978)**  An Act giving the UK government the power to take action over any goods that might bring a risk of death, injury or disease to the public. In certain areas regulations exist, e.g. gas, electric and oil fires, children's clothes, toys, electrical goods, prams and cosmetics. But local **Trading Standards Officers** are able to stop traders selling any dangerous goods even if there are no particular regulations about them. The **Consumer Protection Act (1987)** allows consumers to sue firms producing defective goods. The sale of food and drugs is covered by separate legislation. *See* **Food Safety Act**.

**Consumers' Association** The largest of the private UK **pressure groups** that aim to protect the interests of the consumer. It was set up in 1957 and produces the publication *Which?* This contains the results of extensive consumer tests on a wide range of consumer products and services, with special emphasis on the safety and reliability of products as well as their value for money. The Association also attempts to influence government legislation about the consumer by suggesting new areas where protection might be useful or areas where existing laws need to be improved.

**contribution** The surplus of **sales revenue** over **variable costs** which contributes to paying **fixed costs**. *See* **break-even**.

**contribution cost** *See* **marginal cost**.

**cooperative** A type of business organization with **limited liability** for the owners, but where each owner or member only holds one share in the business and therefore only has one vote in controlling the company. There are three main types of cooperative – consumer cooperatives, worker cooperatives and marketing co-operatives. The most successful examples of this type of organization have been consumer cooperatives, based on the idea that it is the customers who are the members of the society and that the profits are distributed in proportion to the value of purchases. The Co-operative Retail Society and the Co-operative Wholesale Society are important elements of the retail and distributive sector in the UK. Less successful have been attempts to establish worker cooperatives where the owners are the workforce. Large-scale employee cooperatives have suffered from a lack of capital as a financial base, and from a lack of management skill. Smaller-scale worker cooperatives have been more likely to survive, for example marketing cooperatives which have been set up to overcome problems with the **exports** market.

**corporation tax**    A direct tax levied by the government on the profits of all **limited companies**. The profits of sole traders and partnerships are taxed through **income tax**. Businesses pay tax on profits earned in the previous year, and there are allowances that they can claim which reduce the amount of tax that they are liable for. By lowering the level of corporation tax the government should encourage more **investment** by business as companies are able to retain a larger amount of **profit**.

**costs**  The money a business spends in order to produce **goods** and **services** for its customers. One way of classifying the costs of a business is to relate them to the output or sales of the firm.

*Variable costs* are those which vary directly with the output or sales of the business, e.g. raw materials, direct wages.

*Semivariable costs* are those which do vary with output or sales, but not in direct proportion, e.g. electricity bills, heating costs and telephone bills. These costs are often treated as **fixed costs**.

*Fixed costs* are those which remain unchanged whatever the level of output or sales, e.g. rent and rates, interest charges, salaries.

Costs are important because the level of **profit** depends upon the difference between the price of a good and the *unit cost* of producing that good.

**cost benefit analysis**  A way of considering a project by taking into account the **social costs** and **social benefits** of that project. This would include both the financial costs and revenue for the project as well as the wider costs and benefits borne by society as a whole. Such an analysis is employed when the government is considering a major project such as the Channel Tunnel. This would consider, among other things, the costs of building and maintaining the tunnel, the increased traffic on the roads of Kent and the loss of countryside;

as well as the increased revenue from people using the tunnel, the greater employment for those living in the area, and the increased business for local traders. The major problem with carrying out such an analysis is finding some way to give a monetary value to costs and benefits that have no immediate monetary element.

**cost-plus pricing**    The basis of a pricing decision. The costs of production are calculated and then a percentage mark-up is added to make sure a profit is made. For example, an article costs £10 to make. With a 20% mark-up the price will be £12.

**Council Tax**    A charge made by the local authority to cover the cost of local services. The Tax is based on the property's market price in April 1991 and the number of people in the household. Businesses continue to pay the **business rate** which is based on the rateable value of the premises. The rateable value is fixed by the Inland Revenue and a charge per £ is set by central government, for example 75p in the £.

**craft union**    The oldest type of **trade union**, where the members are skilled workers drawn from one particular trade. Therefore members might come from a number of different industries. Entry to the craft would be by an **apprenticeship** scheme to train those entering the trade. The Amalgamated Union of Engineering Workers, first established in the 19th century, is an example of such a union. With the decline in the number of skilled workers as a proportion of the total workforce, such craft unions now recruit semiskilled workers. Many of the smaller craft unions, such as the Plumbers' and the Electricians' Unions, have merged together to form larger skilled groupings.

**credit**   The practice of allowing a fixed period of time in which to pay for a good or service. In most industries, credit is received from suppliers and given to customers with the usual period for payment at three months. This is known as **trade credit**. Increasingly, credit is also being given to consumers by retail outlets which have in the past concentrated on cash sales. This is *consumer credit*. Banks also provide credit to customers in the form of **loans** and **overdrafts**. This is *bank credit*. The cost of credit is the **interest rate** that someone pays the **creditor** when the debt is repaid.

**credit card**   A card for **consumers** that makes it easier to buy goods on **credit**. A customer can use the card for many different purchases in many different outlets, and the customer receives a monthly statement of all the credit they have built up. This can be paid off in 25 days with no interest, or payment can be made in instalments with a rate of interest charged which is higher than for a loan or overdraft. A shop card has more limited use as it can only be used for purchases in one shop or chain of shops.

**creditor**     Someone to whom an individual or business owes money. For example, if a restaurant buys all their meat from a local butcher and is given a period of **credit**, the butcher becomes the trade creditor of the restaurant. If the restaurant has a **bank loan** the bank becomes a creditor. Creditors appear as a **current liability** on the **balance sheet** of a business. If creditors believe that a business is facing problems, then they might call for their money to be repaid, or start proceedings to recover some of their debts.

**current account**     A facility offered by **commercial banks** which allows customers to use cheques and debit cards to make payments for purchases. The banks are able to transfer funds from one bank account to another by way of the clearing system. This has reduced the amount of cash that has needed to be held by individuals and businesses. For example in many cases wages are paid directly into the employee's bank account. In most banks, provided the account is in credit, there is no charge made by the bank for current account transactions. If a customer wishes to draw out more money than is in the current account for a short period, then an **overdraft** is created on which the customer pays interest.

**current asset**     An **asset** that a business owns, i.e. an item that is either **cash** or is likely to be turned into cash in the course of normal trading activities within the next twelve months. Current assets include **stock**, made up of raw materials, work in progress and finished **goods**; money owed to the business by **debtors**; and cash which is both cash in the till and money held in the **current account** at a bank. A business will need sufficient current assets to be able to meet its **current liabilities** and its regular expenses, but will not want too great a level of current assets as the funds could be put to more profitable use.

**current liability**    An item that a business owes to a **creditor** that is likely to be paid back within a year. They are the debts that a business incurs during the course of normal trading activities. They will include **trade credit**, i.e. money owed for the supply of **goods**; bank **overdraft**; **dividends** proposed but not yet paid to **shareholders** and **taxation** due to be paid to the Government in the next year. A business will need to ensure that it has enough **working capital** to be able to meet these short-term debts, as the creditors might want them to be repaid quickly or might not renew the credit. *Compare* **current asset**. *See also* **long-term liability**.

**curriculum vitae (cv)**    A brief recent history of a person stating personal details, the school or college they attended, their qualifications, work experiences and personal interests. It can also give details of referees, prepared to give that person a reference.

**customs and excise duties**   Specific **indirect taxes** paid when **goods** or **services** are purchased or traded. Customs Duties, also known as **tariffs**, are taxes on imported products. Excise Duties are taxes raised on specific products such as petrol, tobacco and alcohol – products which people are likely to continue to demand despite having to pay an extra tax. The majority of such indirect taxes are likely to be passed on by businesses in the form of higher prices for the consumer to pay. Such taxes are imposed in order to raise government revenue for its own spending, and, in some cases, to discourage the public from buying the product.

**cv**   *See* **curriculum vitae**.

# D

**Data Protection Act (1998)**   A law passed to ensure that information kept manually or on computer about individuals, e.g. in a **database**, should be held and used lawfully, should be accurate and not too extensive, and should be held only for a reasonable amount of time.

**database**   A computer program which enables a large amount of information to be stored. It contains records made up of a series of fields of information. A company might keep a database of its customers. The advantage of a computer database is that the computer can search and sort the information very quickly, far faster than any manual search.

**day release**   A system whereby employees are given time during the working week to attend a local college or training centre to study for a qualification **off-the-job** which will help them in their employment. In the past, employees were expected to study for vocational or professional examinations in their spare time, but today many employers, within a training scheme, allow their employees paid time off for these studies.

**debenture**   A long-term **loan** to a company which carries a fixed rate of interest and a repayment date.

It differs from a share in that it is not permanent and the holder receives **interest** rather than **dividend**, and is not a part-owner of the business. Debenture interest is a **fixed cost** for a business and must be paid whether or not the company makes a profit. The issue of debentures as a source of finance for industry has declined in recent years. *See also* **long-term liability**.

**debtor**   A business or individual that owes money to another business or individual, in return for **goods** or **services** provided on **credit**. Debtors are people who owe a business money and are treated as **current assets** of the business. It is important for a business not to let the proportion of debtors to total sales revenue rise too quickly, as they may find that some of the debtors are not able to pay and thus become **bad debts**. The business might also face a cash shortage if there is a high number of debtors.

**decentralization**   *See* **centralization**.

**deindustrialization**   The process in an economy whereby the **primary** and **secondary production** sectors start to decline and the **tertiary production** sector becomes bigger. It indicates a decline in the manufacturing base of the economy. In the UK, for example, between 1974 and 1984 output in the tertiary sector of the economy grew four times as fast as

in the primary and secondary sectors; employment
in the tertiary sector also increased by over a million
while employment in the other sectors fell by
three million.

**delegation**   The passing down of authority in an
organization from a person to a subordinate lower
down the **chain of command**. As one person cannot do
all jobs there needs to be some delegation of work and
authority in an organization. Delegation helps to give
those at a lower level more experience and makes their
work more interesting and motivating (*see* **motivation**).
It should also make the organization more responsive to
the needs of customers. However, the person
delegating the authority has still to keep overall
responsibility for decisions, and needs to ensure that the
subordinate person is capable of carrying out the task.
A marketing manager thus might delegate authority for
running an advertising campaign to one of the
advertising staff, but must keep the final responsibility
for that campaign.

**demand**   The quantity of goods or services that
buyers are willing and able to buy at a particular price
over a period of time. It can be represented by a
*demand curve* which shows how a consumer's demand
may react to a change in the price of a product. In the
diagrams overleaf, as the price falls from $P_0$ to $P_2$
demand will expand as consumers buy more of a

product; as the price rises from $P_0$ to $P_1$ demand will contract as a consumer will buy less of a product.

Demand will also be influenced by other factors, for example the income of customers, the prices of complementary and substitute goods and the tastes and preferences of customers. Changes in any of these factors

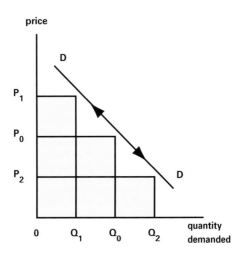

**demand** (a) The demand curve.

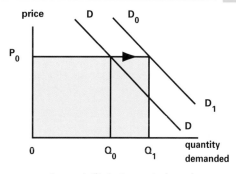

***demand*** *(b) An increase in demand.*

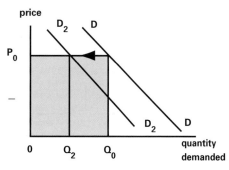

***demand*** *(c) A decrease in demand.*

would cause an increase or decrease in demand. This would be represented on the demand curve by a shift to the right or left. This is shown in graphs (b) and (c). This economic model of demand in a **market** would help a business to see how their customers might behave when faced with changes in prices or other factors. How responsive **consumers** are will vary between different product markets, with some of the factors more important in one market than in another.

For example, price is important in petrol sales and income will be important in car sales. Businesses might also attempt to create or change demand for their products by the use of various **marketing** techniques.

**democratic leadership**   A style of **leadership** in organizations which attempts to involve everyone in a group in decision-making. Such a leader is less likely to command or order than in **autocratic leadership**, but is more likely to discuss and ask for ideas from the group, and come to decisions with which the whole group agrees. Democratic leadership would be suitable for a team working together to develop a product or a marketing campaign, or for a meeting where a group is trying to solve a problem.

**deposit account**   A facility offered by a bank or other financial institution where the money held on account by a business or individual earns an amount of interest which is added to the sum. This rate is set in line with other **interest rates** but will be lower than the rate which a business pays for an **overdraft** or **loan.** Banks and building societies now offer a range of deposit accounts to customers with varying rates of interest depending upon the amount invested and the length of time it is invested. A business will consider the interest it can earn on deposit when looking at other ways of using its money such as buying a machine; the lost interest on the funds would be the **opportunity cost** of such a project.

**depreciation**    A term given to the reduction in value of fixed assets like machinery due to age, wear and tear, or obsolescence as new technology is introduced. An accountant will gradually reduce the value of an asset on the **balance sheet** to scrap value at the end of its expected life, and at the same time reduce the profit figure of the business. Thus depreciation is a **fixed cost** of business. This ensures that the cost of the machine is matched to the revenue that machine earns over its whole lifetime.

The two main methods of calculating depreciation are the *straight line method* and the *reducing balance method*. The straight line method reduces the value of the asset by an equal amount each year using the following formula:

$$\text{Annual Depreciation} = \frac{\text{Cost of Asset} - \text{Scrap Value}}{\text{estimated years of useful life}}$$

e.g. a machine costs £10,000, has an estimated useful life of 8 years and a scrap value of £2,000.

$$\text{Annual Depreciation} = \frac{10,000 - 2,000}{8} = £1,000$$

The reducing balance method reduces the value of the asset by a fixed percentage of its net value every year of its useful life. This method reduces the value by a greater amount in the earlier years which is more realistic for vehicles and machinery.

For example, a van costs £10,000 and is to be depreciated by 20% a year.

Depreciation at the end of the first year = 20% of £10,000 = £2,000.

Depreciation at the end of the second year = 20% of £8,000 = £1,600.

**desk research**   *See* **secondary data**.

**Development Area**    An **Assisted Area** which has a
very high level of long-term unemployment and needs
assistance more urgently than an **Intermediate Area**.

**differential pricing**    *See* **price discrimination**.

**direct costs**    The costs which are allocated
specifically to a product, machine or department in a
business, and which will increase or decrease in relation
to the output of that section. Raw materials and **labour**
costs such as wages and **overtime** payments are usually
easy to allocate, but costs such as lighting, heating and
telephone bills might also be linked to a particular area
of a business, and therefore be treated as direct.
*Compare* **indirect costs**.

**direct tax**    The tax that a government raises
on the basis of the income of an individual or company.
The most important example is *income tax,* a tax
on people's wages and salaries. **Corporation tax** is a
direct tax on the profits of businesses. Together with
**indirect taxes**, direct taxes provide the revenue from
which the government can finance its expenditure
programme. *See* **taxation**.

**discount**    A reduction in the price of a **good** or
**service**; often expressed as a percentage. It is given to
customers who buy in bulk, or who pay in cash, or who
are loyal and favoured customers. Businesses use

discounts as a policy to gain a larger market share than competitors. For example, a customer with a bill of £500 who receives 5% discount would pay £475.

**diseconomies of scale**    An increase in **average costs** that may occur as a firm's output is increased beyond a critical point. As businesses grow in size there are various factors which lead to lower average costs known as **economies of scale**. But beyond a certain size, these average costs might start to rise again as diseconomies of scale start to set in. It becomes more difficult to administer and organize larger-scale enterprises, and the bureaucracy needed becomes expensive. The **chain of command** might be longer and a breakdown in industrial relations might result. Outside the business, transport costs increase due to congestion, and increased pollution might occur.

**dismissal**    The ending, by an employer, of the contract of employment with an employee either because the employee has broken the contract in some way, or when a fixed-term contract is not renewed. Dismissal must be for a specific reason, i.e. misconduct, inability to do the job or **redundancy**, which is when the job no longer exists. The employee must receive a reasonable period of notice before the dismissal occurs. If an employee is dismissed for no good reason or if too little notice is given, then this might be an **unfair dismissal** and the employee can appeal to an industrial tribunal for compensation or for reinstatement.

**distributed profit**  The amount of **profit** after tax that a company may distribute to **shareholders**. Once a company has arrived at its net profit figure for a year, with all **costs** and expenses including tax and interest allowed for, then the **board of directors** must decide what proportion of that profit will be kept in the business to be used for expansion – **retained profit** – and what proportion will be distributed to the shareholders – distributed profit. For example, the net profit of a large company in 1997 was £1,566m of which £930m was retained and £636m was distributed. It would have been distributed in the form of **dividends** on each share owned. It is up to the board to decide how much, if anything, to distribute to the shareholders.

**distribution**  The *place* element of the **marketing mix**, i.e. the means by which the product is delivered to the **consumer** at the right place and at the right time. It would involve decisions about which **channel of distribution** to use, which method of transport to use, and how regular and large deliveries to customers will be. The other elements of the mix will be influenced by and will influence these decisions. If a long channel is chosen then the price of the final product will be raised. If road transport is chosen, then bulk delivery will be more expensive for some products. The image which is created for a product by **advertising** might be ruined if the wrong outlets are chosen for sales.

**diversification**   The practice of moving into a product or **market** area which is different from the one in which a particular business is already established. Thus a drinks manufacturer might purchase a television company as a way of diversifying. Businesses do this in order to continue growing, to spread risks over a wider number of markets and to increase their profitability. Problems might occur if the business does not have any expertise in the new market, if there is a sudden downturn in the new business, or if a business overextends itself given its financial base. Diversification can happen through natural growth or by **merger** and **takeover**.

**dividend**   The share of the **profits** which a business pays to its **shareholders**. It is a reward to the shareholders for investing their money in the business. **Preference shares** pay a fixed dividend provided a profit is made, while the dividend for **ordinary shares** is decided each year by the **board of directors** and depends upon how much they wish to distribute of their profits. Preference shareholders receive their dividends before the ordinary shareholders. The share of profits that a shareholder receives through their dividend is one of the features that attracts investors to buy or hold shares. Thus a business announcing high dividends is likely to be more attractive to investors than one with low dividends.

**division of labour**    A system of specialization in tasks. In any economy, resources are employed to do different specialist tasks in order to increase the production of that economy. This process of specialization is known as the 'division of labour'. At a national level, this means that some resources are devoted to **primary production**, some are devoted to manufacturing and some to the service sector. At an international level, countries specialize in the production of some **goods** and trade these with other countries. At a factory level, tasks are divided up into small jobs with individual workers learning only those skills needed in one small part of the production process. Thus, while the division of labour helps increase production, it may make each job less skilled and less interesting. Even at a national level, too much reliance on one product might lead to problems for a country if there is a decline in the demand for that product.

**downsizing**    A method of improving **profits** by reducing the number of employees and increasing the **productivity** of the smaller workforce.

Downsizing usually tends to be a short-term solution because the remaining workforce cannot easily cope with future growth and the increased work load.

# E

**e-commerce**   Conducting business over the **Internet** or through other electronic networks, such as **Viewdata**. E-commerce is increasing in importance, because it is a relatively inexpensive way for businesses to be in contact with their customers. It also offers businesses access to a broadly dispersed marketplace, providing access to any business or individual around the world with a PC and internet access.

**economic growth**   The increase in a country's real output over a period of time. A country's output is measured by its gross national product, and 'real growth' means growth that is not just caused by changes in prices. It is a basic indicator showing how well a country's economy is performing. The main features that cause such long-term growth include the following:

- (a) Increases in natural resources, e.g. the development of North Sea oil.
- (b) Increases in the production of capital goods, e.g. firms using more advanced technology in production.
- (c) Improvements in technology, e.g. new discoveries and new processes.
- (d) Improvements in the human resource, e.g. a better educated workforce.

There are social costs to economic growth, for example, the costs of pollution, or the problems of overcrowding in cities which would reduce the benefits of such growth.

**economies of scale**   Those factors which, as a business grows, allow the **average costs** of that business to fall. A large number of internal economies of scale have been identified:

**Technical Economies, e.g.**

- division of labour

- using larger plant and machinery

- savings in large volumes by using mass production

**Marketing Economies, e.g.**

- bulk buying of raw materials and components

- sharing costs of advertising

- bulk delivery of finished goods

- sales promotion over several markets

---

> **Financial Economies, e.g.**
>
> - greater financial resources
> - wider source of finance available
> - risk spread over more products
> - lower interest rates available from lenders
>
> **Administrative Economies, e.g.**
>
> - more specialized management
> - computer systems in offices

---

*Compare* **diseconomies of scale**. *See also* **external economies of scale**.

**Education and Employment, Department for (DfEE)**   A large UK government ministry under the Secretary of State for Employment, which oversees the government's education, manpower and employment policies. In addition to the responsibility for standards of education, DfEE is responsible for promoting employment nationally and regionally, manning Jobcentres, employment and training schemes (through the Training Agency), industrial training, youth employment and health and safety and welfare at work through the Factory Inspectors. Its work in **industrial relations** is the responsibility of **ACAS**. In devising its policies it consults with the **TUC** and **CBI**

representatives, as well as working with employment ministers from other countries in the **European Union**.

**electronic mail or email** The transmission and distribution of information through personal computers linked to the telephone system, which allows subscribers to send a message directly to another subscriber that will appear in their electronic mail box.

**electronic point of sale (EPOS)** A system used in retailing which links the cash desk to a computer. Each product sold has a bar code which is read by the computer using a light-sensitive pen or scanning window. The price of the good is then printed out for the customer and assistant while at the same time the computer records what has been sold and adjusts the stock level accordingly. Thus the checkout provides the company with information on the sales of each product line. It can also create purchaser profiles, collecting information on how customers shop. Such a system is common in large supermarkets, chain stores and department stores.

**employers' associations** Groupings of employers from the same industry or trade who represent employers' interests in discussions and negotiations with unions, other industries and the government. The association might take part directly in wage negotiations with trade unions to reach a national agreement

covering the whole industry or trade. It would also help
members to sort out particular labour relations
problems or disputes. The Engineering Employers'
Federation and the Federation of Road Hauliers are two
important examples.

**Employment Acts**    A series of acts passed by the
UK government which introduced major elements of
legislation in the way **industrial relations** are organized.
The legislation covers the following areas:

- Unions are required to hold secret strike ballots
  before taking any industrial action.

- Individuals have a right not to join a closed shop,
  and can appeal for unfair dismissal if they lose
  their job for refusing to join.

- Secondary picketing and secondary action are
  made illegal.

- The legal immunity of trade unions, which had
  existed since 1906, is lifted if their industrial action
  was unlawful, i.e. not in direct pursuit of a trade
  dispute. Unions can now be sued for unlawful
  industrial action.

- Workers dismissed by employers for taking
  industrial action cannot claim unfair dismissal.

The Employment Acts represent a considerable reduction in the freedom of trade unions to pursue industrial action. *See also* **Trade Union Act**.

**Employment Relations Act (1999)**　An act that gives a union the right of recognition if a majority of workers in the workplace support it. It also gives workers the right to be accompanied by a union representative during disciplinary proceedings.

**enterprise zones**　Poor inner-city areas which were chosen by the UK government between 1981 and 1984 to receive special assistance and help. In these small, depressed areas, businesses were encouraged to set up and create new jobs by various incentives such as 100% grants for new buildings, grants for new machinery and exemption from business rates. Each zone received support for 10 years. The aim was to regenerate economic activity in these areas where old industries had declined.

**entrepreneur**　The risk taker in an organization, the entrepreneur is traditionally seen as the owner/manager of a business. As well as putting up the **finance** for the business, this person also runs the business and in return receives a reward in the form of **profit**. As a business grows, there is likely to be a division between ownership and management, so that the role of the entrepreneur is reduced. In recent years the government has tried to encourage entrepreneurs to set up and run their own businesses as an alternative to unemployment, providing start-up grants to help this process. The number of such small businesses has grown although many also fail after a short period. Well-known entrepreneurs include Richard Branson (Virgin Records) and Anita Roddick (Body Shop).

**environmental audit**   A review of the environmental effects of a business's operations. It will consider the impact on the environment of all business practices, monitor compliance with regulations, and explore ways to minimize pollution and waste and increase energy efficiency. It will establish environment-friendly policies. Environmental audits often suggest substantial cost savings and also contribute to a positive public image.

**Environmental Health Officer**   The Environmental Health Office is a local government department with responsibility for enforcing the **Food Safety Act (1990)**. The Environmental Health Officer will inspect premises where food is being prepared to make sure that conditions are hygienic, food is correctly stored and staff are properly trained to deal with food. This department will deal with consumers' complaints, such as finding a snail in a packet of frozen peas, and prosecute when needed. The Environmental Health Officer also investigates cases of food poisoning. The Environmental Health Office reports to the Food Standards Agency. *See* **Food Standards Act.**

**Equal Opportunities Commission**    A body set up under the 1975 Sex Discrimination Act to try and ensure that there is no discrimination on the grounds of sex in employment or promotion opportunities. It also seeks to watch over the **Equal Pay Act** to ensure that men and women receive equal pay for equal work. The Commission can investigate individual cases of **sex discrimination** as well as reporting on employers who they feel could improve their policies on equal opportunities. It can also act against advertisements that might lead to sexual discrimination. Thus if a woman felt that she had been unfairly overlooked for promotion just because she is a woman, she might appeal for support to the Commission in pursuing a case against the employers.

**Equal Pay Act**    An Act passed by the UK Parliament in 1970 and then amended in 1984. This Act aimed to cut out wage inequality between men and women (*see also* **Equal Opportunities Commission**). It also covers other conditions of work like holiday provision. The Act says that where a woman is employed in similar or equivalent work to a man in the same employment, then she should receive the same pay and conditions of employment as the man. Disputes about equal pay can be brought to an **industrial tribunal**. The Act was amended in 1984 to resolve problems in deciding where men and women are doing different jobs which are of equal value.

**equities**  A general term for any claims on a business by people who have contributed funds to that business to allow it to acquire assets. Thus all **liabilities** and **capital** would be included as such claims. In popular usage, however, equities mean the **ordinary shares** of a business, as these form the part that is left over when all the liabilities of a firm have been met if a business goes into **liquidation**.

**European Union (EU)**  A group of 15 member countries: Austria, Belgium, Denmark, Eire, Finland, France, Germany, Greece, Holland, Italy, Luxembourg, Portugal, Spain, Sweden and the United Kingdom. It has three important elements. It is a **free trade** area, in that there are no **tariffs** between the countries on exports. It has a Common External Tariff against countries outside the community, although with exemptions for poorer countries. It has certain common economic policies covering agriculture (*see* **Common Agricultural Policy**), energy, a European Monetary System, regional problems and transport. It is controlled by the European Commission and a directly elected European Parliament, although the ultimate power of decision-making lies with the Council of Ministers.

**exchange rate**   The rate at which one currency trades for another currency on the foreign-exchange market. Businesses that are involved in international trade will be interested in changes in the exchange rate because they will affect the prices paid for imports and exports. A falling exchange rate will help exporters as it will make their **goods** cheaper overseas. It will make imported goods more expensive. A rising exchange rate will help importers, as it will lower the price of imported goods, but exporters will face rising prices for their goods.

Other businesses in an economy will also be affected. Those competing against imported goods will benefit from a falling exchange rate but lose competitiveness with a rising one. Those businesses using imported raw materials will find their costs of production rising with a falling exchange rate, but falling with a rising exchange rate.

**excise duty**   *See* **indirect tax**.

**exports**   **Goods** or **services** produced in one country but sold in another. In the UK, the major export earnings come from oil, manufactured goods and financial services. However, **imports** in raw materials and increasingly in manufactured goods often result in a deficit in the UK on its **balance of payments**. Exports are important because they allow a country to earn foreign exchange which can then be used for buying imports from abroad. Many less developed countries find that they have insufficient exports to be able to afford the imported goods they need to develop further.

**external economies of scale**    Types of **economies of scale** that arise for a group of firms, or a whole industry, rather than for an individual firm. They occur as a result of the firms being located or organized together, and cause the costs of production of all the firms involved to be reduced. Examples include:

- the sharing of transport facilities by firms, such as a rail link or harbour

- technological research and development by an industry that is then shared between all the firms in that industry

- training facilities and courses that are provided for the whole industry

- suppliers being located close to a group of firms that produce similar products

# F

**factors of production**   The resources which are employed to allow production of **goods** and **services** to take place; the **inputs** for the production process. They are divided into four types: **land** is the natural resource, including the minerals in the earth and under the sea; **labour** is the human resource; **capital** is the man-made resource, which includes machinery, tools, buildings; and *enterprise* involves the skills of taking risks and decisions.

Different countries will use these resources in different quantities depending upon their availability; in countries where labour is plentiful production will be **labour-intensive**; in countries where capital is plentiful, production will be more **capital-intensive**.

**Fair Trading Act (1973)**   An Act that set up the **Office of Fair Trading**, whose Director-General was given powers to oversee the trading activities of organizations. The Director is able to forbid any trade practice which misleads consumers about the quality of **goods**, about their rights, or which puts the consumer under pressure. The Office is also responsible for preventing any restrictive trade practices, and can report organizations to the **Monopolies and Mergers**

**Commission** if it thinks their activities are against the public interest. Its measures were extended by the **Competition Act**.

**field research**   *See* **primary data**.

**finance, sources of**   There are various internal and external sources of finance that a business can employ when seeking to fund its operations.

Some of the important institutional sources for business finance include the **Stock Exchange** for share finance, **commercial banks** for **loans** or **overdrafts**, **merchant banks** for loans and **venture capital**; **building societies** for **mortgages**; finance houses for **hire purchase** and **leasing** arrangements, and the government for loans and grants.

**finance, uses of**   The ways in which a business employs the finance that it raises. This is represented on the **balance sheet** by the **assets** of a business. The use to which a business puts its finance needs to be matched to the type of finance that is being used. For the purchase of **fixed assets** it will use **capital** or long-term finance, as the payback period for such assets will be some time in the future. For the purchase of **current assets**, it will use short-term funds such as **trade credit** or a bank **overdraft** as it will expect to turn the assets into cash quite quickly. If too much of a business's short-term finance is tied up in long-term investments, then it might face liquidity problems if its short-term **creditors** wish for early payment.

**fiscal policy**    An economic policy pursued by a government that regulates the use of government expenditure and **taxation**. The government can affect the level of economic activity in a country by changing the amount it spends, and by changing the amount it raises in taxation to pay for this spending. If the government wishes to expand the economy, in order to reduce **unemployment**, then it can increase government expenditure on **goods** and **services** and reduce the levels of taxation. Both of these policies will encourage consumer spending, and businesses will find an increased demand for their products.

If the government wishes to contract the level of economic activity, perhaps because the level of inflation is rising, then it can reduce its expenditure and increase the level of taxation. These policies will discourage consumer spending in the economy and businesses will find a reduced demand for their products.

**fixed assets**    Items that a business owns which make a long-term contribution to the activity of a business. For a manufacturing company they might consist of the factory, the machinery and tools used in the factory, office equipment and vehicles. Not all fixed assets are physical items however; a business might own important **patents** or **trademarks**, and might also have an amount of goodwill for being an established business. Such assets are known as *intangible assets*, in contrast to the physical ones such as plant and machinery.

**fixed costs or overheads**   Those **costs** of a business which remain unchanged at whatever the level of output the business is producing and selling over a period of time. Such costs might include **rent** and rates paid, interest charges and **depreciation** of machinery owned by the business. Some salaries might also be regarded as fixed costs as some employees will be needed even when a firm is not producing. A fixed cost does not change as **output** or sales change, therefore the greater the sales of a business, the better it is able to cover its fixed costs. However, if sales fall, a business might find itself making a loss as fixed costs still have to be paid. *Compare* **variable costs**.

**flow production**   A production process which is based upon a line of machinery which operates virtually continuously, producing very large quantities of similar products. The assembly cars, TVs and refrigerators are good examples of the process, but such a system can also be applied to processes like brewing, paper production or oil refining. Such a method of production makes heavy use of machinery and will thus have higher setting-up costs (*see* **capital-intensive**). However, once operating to full capacity it will have low **average costs**. Products made are likely to be of similar design with a small product range, and will need to be sold in large quantities on a regular basis. A criticism of this type of production is that the skills required of the people working in the production line are low, with each job being repetitive. *Compare* **batch production, job production**.

**Food and Drugs Act (1955)**    *See* **Food Safety Act (1990)**.

**Food Safety Act (1990)**    This act updates and replaces the Food and Drugs Act (1955). The law protects the consumer by making it illegal to sell food which has not been prepared under hygienic conditions. It is also illegal to sell food which is not fit for human consumption. This act also sets out guidelines for labelling of food items. Prepacked food must be clearly labelled with an accurate description of the food, an accurate list of ingredients, a 'sell-by date' and, where appropriate, the length of time it can be stored in a refrigerator or freezer. The food must also match the description. For example, to be described as 'strawberry' jam, the jam must contain a certain amount of strawberries. This law is enforced by the **Environmental Health Officer**.

**Food Standards Act (1999)** Legislation establishing the Food Standards Agency, charged with protecting consumer interests in relation to food safety and standards. It enforces and monitors food safety and conducts research, issuing the results both to the Government and to the public. The **Environmental Health Officer** reports to the Food Standards Agency.

**formal organization** The way people in an organization are regulated in a **hierarchy** in order to achieve the objectives of their organization. This would be represented in the form of an **organization chart**, rulebooks, regulations, etc. All those help to define the position and role of the people in an organization in relation to each other. People will also create an **informal organization** made up of friendship groups, and this can often cut across the formal system, producing objectives different to those of the formal organization.

**four Ps** *See* **marketing mix**.

**franchising** A method of selling that has become increasingly common in the UK and Europe within the **retailing** sector. A large company gives permission to a person to market their product in a certain area in return for that person paying a sum of money to use the product name.

The person operating the franchise is self-employed, but will be supplied with equipment, training and in some cases the product to be sold, by the franchisor. In return the large company will receive a share of the profits. Examples of franchises include McDonalds, Benetton, Prontaprint and Thorntons.

**free market economy**    A type of economy where decisions about what to produce, how to produce and in what quantities, are made by the **market**, in response to **demand** and **supply**. All the **factors of production** are privately owned, and individuals will organize them to produce the **goods** which are most wanted by the **consumer** as reflected in the **price** that the consumer is willing to pay for the goods. The government has no role to play in regulating the way the market operates. In the US, much of the economy operates on a free market system, but the government does play a role in the provision of defence and education. In the **European Union** governments play a larger role, so these are **mixed economies**. *Compare* **planned economy**.

**free trade**    The exchange of **goods** and **services** between countries, without any barriers being erected which might alter the direction or quantity of that trade. Such barriers might be **tariffs**, **quotas** or **nontariff barriers**. Within the **European Union**, there is free trade between the 15 members in the sense that there are no tariffs or quotas. Changes in 1992 eliminated those barriers and created the so-called *single market.* Free trade should allow countries to enjoy the benefits of specialization and growth, but for developing countries it might prove to be harmful, as they may be swamped by **imports** from developed countries which might prevent their own industries from growing. Thus they might impose trade barriers to protect their infant industries.

**fringe benefit**  A benefit, or perk, which an employee receives in addition to their wage. Examples of fringe benefits include private health insurance, free uniform, company car, discounts on company products, and free or subsidized meals. Fringe benefits are intended to increase employees' **motivation**.

# G

**general union**   A type of **trade union** which recruits its members from across a number of industries. It represents semiskilled and unskilled workers in a variety of occupations. For example, the Transport and General Workers Union represents farm workers, car assembly workers, dockers, and school cleaners. Members of general unions may be working alongside members from **craft** and **white-collar unions** in the same organization, so management of that organization will often have to negotiate with representatives from a variety of unions.

**goods**   A general term used to represent the wide variety of tangible items which are produced as a result of economic activity. Goods are classified as either **consumer goods** or **capital goods**.

**government expenditure**   The money which the government spends each year in the provision of **goods** and **services** and on **investment** in the country. The major items of expenditure are on defence, the Health Service, social security, education and grants to local authorities. Such expenditure is paid for out of **taxation** and borrowing. The government forms an important part of the UK economy and increases or decreases in its level of expenditure can have an important effect upon the level of economic activity in the country. *See* **fiscal policy**.

**grievance**   A dispute that arises between an individual worker or group of workers, and the **management** of a firm. It might concern, for example, the disciplining of an individual worker for lateness, or a disagreement over bonus payments with a section of workers. Most industries and companies have a grievance procedure which workers can follow if they feel that they have been wronged. The first stage might involve discussion with the foreman, who would then take the matter up with the departmental manager, and so on until the matter is resolved. Only when this procedure has been completed – and with no agreement reached – would **industrial action** or **arbitration** be considered.

**gross pay**   An individual's earnings for work done, before any deductions have been made for income tax, national insurance, etc. Where workers have an hourly rate, gross pay is calculated by adding **overtime** and **bonus payments** to basic pay (number of hours worked x hourly rate of pay). After deductions, the pay is known as **net pay**.

**gross profit**   The figure obtained on the profit-and-loss account when the *cost of goods sold* is deducted from the *sales revenue* of a business. It does not take into account any of the expenses of running a business such as wages, distribution costs or administration costs. The example shows how gross profit would be calculated for a small manufacturing company.

| Trading Account for Stephenson Ltd. | | |
|---|---|---|
| | £ | £ |
| Sales revenue (turnover) | | 100,000 |
| Less cost of goods sold | | |
| Opening stock | 24,000 | |
| Add purchases | 60,000 | |
| | 84,000 | |
| Less closing stock | 30,000 | |
| = Cost of goods sold | | 54,000 |
| Gross profit | | 46,000 |

This is the basic measure of **profit** for a business. Once other expenses, interest and **taxation** are deducted from this figure, **net profit** will be considerably smaller.

# H

**Health and Safety at Work Act (1974)**   A law which ensures that all employees have a degree of protection against having an accident or contracting a disease at their place of work. Before 1974, the legislation that existed did not cover all employees or all industries. The main element of the Act is that every employer should ensure the health, safety and welfare at work of his/her employees. If the employer does not do this then he/she can be prosecuted whether or not anyone is injured. Employers are also responsible for the health and safety of other people, e.g. those living near their factory in a case of pollution. The Act set up a Health and Safety Executive, whose inspectors enforce the Act and investigate any breaches of regulations. In addition, each **trade union** in a factory appoints a safety representative who carries out regular inspections of the workplace to investigate possible health and safety hazards.

**Herzberg, Frederick**   A researcher who, during the 1960s, investigated what motivated people at work. Using research in a number of organizations he identified two factors:

*motivators*, which are those factors which give workers
    job satisfaction, for example, responsibility,
    promotion prospects, sense of achievement, the
    nature of the job itself;

*hygiene factors*, which could lead to job dissatisfaction if
    they are inadequate, for example, pay, working
    conditions, company rules, relationship with
    management. Hygiene factors can also be referred to
    as 'maintenance factors'.

While the hygiene factors have to be met by
management to avoid job dissatisfaction, they do not
lead to job satisfaction. For this, management have to
create conditions where the **motivation** needs can be
met for the workforce. To do this Herzberg promoted
the concept of **job enrichment**, that is, the reshaping of
jobs to allow responsibility, achievement and recognition
to occur.

**hierarchy    1.** The number of levels of authority in an
organization. In a hierarchy, each superior will have a
clear position with a **span of control** over a number of
subordinates, and each person will have a clear job
description. *See* **organization chart**.
**2.** The **formal organization** as a whole.

**hire purchase (HP)**    A way for **consumers** to buy on
credit, which involves paying a deposit on a product
and then paying off the balance in a series of

instalments. These instalments will cover the price of the **goods**, the interest charged on the whole **loan**, and a service charge to cover administrative costs. This makes HP an expensive method of credit. An important feature is that the ownership of the goods does not pass to the consumer until the final payment is made.

**horizontal merger**   The joining of two companies which operate at the same level of production and produce the same type of product. The merger of Rowntrees and Nestlé, both of which make chocolate, was a horizontal merger. The main advantages of such a merger are that the new company has a larger **market share** and has reduced the number of competitors in the **market**.

Greater **economies of scale** should occur but consumers may be faced with less choice, and therefore such mergers might be investigated by the **Monopolies and Mergers Commission** if too much of a **monopoly** is created. *See* **lateral merger**.

**hot-desking**   A term used to describe workers who are given no fixed desks. Instead, they use any available space when they are in the office. The concept is popular as it enables a very effective use of office space.

# I

**import controls**   Any of the methods that a
government can employ to reduce the level of **imports**
coming into a country in order to reduce a **balance of
payments** deficit or protect domestic business. Methods
include **tariffs**, **quotas**, exchange controls and a variety
of **nontariff barriers** which might discourage imports.
All the members of the **European Union** adopt a
common trading policy to nonmember countries.
For example, the Union imposes trade quotas on the
number of Japanese cars which can be imported into
the EU, and a common external tariff on other Japanese
goods whichever country might import them. Within
the Union itself, however, there are no tariffs or quotas,
and nontariff barriers were removed by the end of 1992.

**imports**   Those **goods** and **services** which are
consumed in one country but which have been
purchased from another country. Imports are
paid for by foreign currency earned by exporters. The
UK has traditionally been an importer of raw materials
and food, but in the last 25 years the import of
manufactured goods has grown as the UK has increased
its trade with other Western European economies.
Manufactured goods are now the largest component
of UK imports, while the **European Union** has

become the most important source of UK imports.
*Compare* **exports**.

**incentive scheme**   A method that employers use to
motivate the workforce, involving financial bonuses if a
certain level of output or sales is achieved. **Fringe
benefits**, such as increased holiday entitlement or
private health care insurance are increasingly being used
as incentives in large organizations. The use of such
incentives assumes that **motivation** will be increased by
external rewards, as reflected in the ideas of **F.W.
Taylor**. These contrast with the views of **Douglas
McGregor**, who believed that motivation is based upon
improving the job itself.

**income tax**   *See* **direct tax**.

**indirect costs or overheads**   Those **costs** which
cannot be directly identified with a particular cost
centre in a factory. The costs of energy used, of
administration, of security and of the wages of office
and support staff might all be difficult to allocate to a
particular product, and therefore may be taken as a
lump-sum cost for the whole business. Accountants
have devised ways of allocating these costs by using a
variety of simple methods; e.g., **rent** and rates might be
allocated by the floor area that a product takes up;
administration cost might be allocated by the number
of people employed on each product. *Compare*

**direct costs**.

**indirect tax**    A source of a government's revenue that is based upon the expenditure of people rather than on their income (*see* **taxation**; compare **direct tax**). Such a tax is paid when goods or services are purchased by **consumers**. The main indirect tax in the UK is the **Value-Added Tax (VAT)**; other indirect taxes, known as *excise duties,* are levied on petrol, alcohol, tobacco and betting. VAT is a tax levied by all members of the **European Union**, to ensure that there is fair competition between goods from different member countries, although not all the countries have the same rate of VAT.

**induction**    Training given to a new employee starting a job. This introduces him or her to colleagues, and provides information about the firm's activities, rules and practices. Induction training aims to help new employees feel comfortable in their new jobs very quickly, and therefore to make a contribution to the firm.

**industrial action**    The activities carried out by a **trade union** in pursuit of an industrial dispute with employers. It occurs when **industrial relations** break down. A **strike** is one example; **work-to-rule**, **overtime bans**, go-slows, **picketing**, **lock-outs** and **boycotts** are others. An employer might also take industrial action by locking out or sacking striking employees. The **Trade Union Act** of 1984 introduced considerable legal controls over the rights of trade unions to pursue industrial action, especially in an unofficial dispute. A secret ballot of those in dispute must take place before industrial action is allowed. Industrial action is no longer that common in the UK; the majority of the workforce will never take part in any industrial action in their working life.

**industrial relations**    The whole range of relationships that exist between managements and their organizations, employees and their organizations, and the government. At its simplest level, it is used to describe the process of **collective bargaining** between **trade unions** and management over pay and working conditions. But it also covers all types of employee/management discussions, including consultation and cooperation. In the UK, emphasis has moved away from national negotiations towards company or plant-level negotiations. When industrial relations break down, then **industrial action** might result. *See* **Employment Acts**.

**industrial tribunals**    Tribunals that were established in 1964 to deal with disputes between individual workers and their employers, including such issues as **unfair dismissal**, **racial** or **sex discrimination**, equal pay or redundancy payments. Such a tribunal is not a formal court, but an informal board made up of representatives from **management** and unions plus a legally qualified third member. The idea of such tribunals is to avoid the formality of court proceedings, although an increasing amount of law is now being passed which is being applied through these tribunals.

**industrial union**    A type of **trade union** which represents all types of worker within one particular industry. In theory such a union might have members for white-collared jobs, skilled jobs, and unskilled jobs. This type of union is not very common in the UK because **craft** and **general unions** have recruited across industries, thus preventing the emergence of only one union in an industry. The National Union of Mineworkers and the National Union of Railwaymen were established as industrial unions, but have not succeeded in covering the whole of their industries. In Germany, industrial unions have been more successful. The recent development of **single-union agreements** in some UK companies suggests a move towards this type of organization.

**inflation**    A progressive increase in the general level of **prices** in an economy. The rate of inflation is the rate at which the general price level is rising. In the case of the prices of **consumer goods**, the **Retail Price Index** is used to measure that rate. For businesses, inflation can cause problems because price rises may make their products less competitive in domestic and world markets. The major causes of inflation have been identified as:

(a) **Cost-push inflation, when rising costs lead to rising prices, which in turn lead to rising costs.**

(b) **Demand-pull inflation, where excessive demand in a sector of the economy pulls up prices, which then pull up costs, and so on.**

The government will try to control inflation using **monetary policy** and/or **fiscal policy**.

**informal organization**   A network of social and friendship groups that exists in an organization separately from the **formal organization**. Informal organizations were first recognized by **G.E. Mayo** in his research. Such groupings might not have the same objectives as the formal organization, and might operate against its interests. Informal groups might have different leaders from those officially in charge and might set themselves different targets from those of the organization. An informal communication network also exists, known as the grapevine.

**information technology (IT)**   The use of computers to store, process, retrieve and communicate information. Personal computers in offices can be used for producing and editing text, **word processing**, and storing and manipulating information in a **database** and **spreadsheet**. There also exist computerized information systems such as Prestel and other **viewdata** systems. Such systems have the advantage of being able to store large amounts of data which can be retrieved quickly. They can help to improve the quality of decision-making in an organization by ensuring that there is more data on which to base a decision. *See also* **internet**.

**infrastructure**   *See* **capital goods**.

**input**   *See* **factors of production**.

**insolvency**   The condition of being unable to meet debts. A company is insolvent when it is unable to meet the demands of all its **creditors** by selling all its **assets** for cash. In such a situation, the creditors would apply for the business to be wound up, and ask for a liquidator to be appointed who could dispose of the assets and pay off the creditors. The company would cease trading, and, when the winding up is complete, cease to exist. *See also* **bankruptcy**.

**intangible assets** *See* **fixed assets.**

**interest rate** The price an individual or business pays for borrowing money. When a sum of money is borrowed, the amount repaid is greater than the amount originally lent; this difference represents the rate of interest, the price that is being paid for the use of that money. There is a range of interest rates in the economy for **loans** which are long and short term, and for different sizes and types of loan. For businesses, higher interest rates tend to discourage new **investment**, and reduce consumer demand because the cost of borrowing is high. Low interest rates encourage new investment, and increase consumer demand as the cost of borrowing is low.

   **Inflation** can also affect how a business reacts to changes in interest rates. As inflation rises, businesses that are borrowing money will find that they will not be paying back in the form of interest as much in real terms as they expected, because the value of the money has declined. If interest rates are 15%, but inflation rises to 10%, then the real rate of interest on money borrowed is only 5%. The **Bank of England** has the power to control interest rates in the UK.

**Intermediate Area** An **Assisted Area** which, in the future, will deteriorate into a **Development Area** unless it is given financial assistance.

**Internet**    An international communications system made up of numerous small computer networks linked by telephone or cable lines. The Internet is used by businesses for **e-commerce**, providing online information on products and services, advertising and retailing opportunities. It is an inexpensive way to reach customers. **Electronic mail** (Email) is also used extensively in business as a means of both external and internal communication.

**investment**    **1.** Individual savings. For example, a family might make an investment by buying unit trusts or by placing money in a building society high-interest account.
**2.** The purchase by a business of new capital or of **capital goods** such as new machinery. In the context of the economy as a whole, investment is the total expenditure by businesses on capital goods, including the building up of **stocks**, and this forms an important element in total expenditure in an economy. Expenditure by the government on **infrastructure** is also a type of investment. Investment, whether by businesses or the individual, represents an alternative to **consumer** expenditure on goods and services.

**invisible trade**    This term used to refer to the import and export of services. Invisibles now appear as 'trade in services' in the **balance of payments**.

**invoice**   A document used to show the record of a purchase by an individual or a business. The invoice will also show the **goods** ordered and purchased, their quantity, their unit and total price, any **value-added tax** being charged on the purchase and any **discount** that is being given. It thus provides a complete record of this part of the transaction between a buyer and a seller.

# J

**JIT**   *See* **just-in-time**.

**job description**   A statement describing the type of work a job involves. It contains the job title, the department or place in the organization, duties and responsibilities. The job description may form the basis of an appraisal, where staff progress is evaluated and staff development needs are identified.

**job enrichment**   The process of trying to make a job more satisfying and motivating for an employee by changing the nature of the job (*see* **motivation**). It is based on **Mayo**'s ideas of human relations management. Some methods of making a job more interesting are shown in the figure on the right.

For example, the job of a **production line** worker might be enriched by making him/her responsible for the **quality control** of the **goods** that are being produced. The aim would be to motivate the worker to produce more and better quality goods. *See also* **quality circles**.

**job production**   A way of organizing **production** where a series of different products is made to customers' orders. Because each order is likely to be

> **Job Rotation**
>
> – varying the tasks carried out
>
> **Job Enlargement**
>
> – increasing tasks in the job
> – lengthening the job
>
> **Job Enrichment**
>
> – increasing complexity and scope of the job
> – more responsibilities
> – more involvement in decision-making

*job enrichment* A comparison of methods aimed at making jobs more interesting.

different, a **batch** or **flow production** system cannot be used. A variety of processes is likely to be involved, and the order each product follows may be different, as will the length of time taken in each process. Such production may involve more skilled work by craft workers as there are likely to be fewer repetitive activities, therefore the **average costs** for each product are likely to be higher. Hand-crafted furniture, jewellery, pottery and clothing are examples of goods produced using this method, where the emphasis is on craftsmanship rather than on quantity of production.

**job satisfaction**  The pleasure a worker experiences from doing his or her job.

**job specification**  *See* **person specification**.

**just-in-time (JIT)**  A principle developed in Japan which involves stocks being delivered to the business 'just-in-time' to be used; the term is used to describe manufacturing and stock control. Just-in-time is an essential feature of lean production when, in order to minimize storage costs, stocks of raw materials and components are not held in the factory store but are delivered to the production line just-in-time to be used. Goods are produced to meet customer demand, and as soon as production is complete they are delivered, reducing the need for storage of finished goods.

A major benefit is an increased **cash flow** with less money tied up in stocks. Problems can arise if there is a sudden increase in customer demand, or if transport difficulties occur; it is possible that bulk buying discounts may be reduced. Large supermarkets also use the just-in-time principle for restocking their shelves.

**Electronic point of sale (EPOS)** stock control means that computerized ordering notifies the regional distribution centre, which dispatches orders just before stocks run out.

# L

**labour**   The human **factor of production**; a resource that is used in production but which is also the reason why production is taking place. Labour is the work which is provided by individuals through their physical skill and effort and intellectual skill and effort. This factor service is provided in return for wages and salaries, which are the rewards for labour. While the amount of labour in an economy is determined by the **labour supply**, the quality of labour is dependent on the level of skills and education in an economy. Thus better training and education can improve the quality of this resource, and therefore improve its contribution as a factor of production.

**labour-intensive**   Where an industry or a particular system of **production** relies on the use of **labour** as a **factor of production**, rather than **capital**. **Service** industries, such as retailing, require large quantities of labour to ensure good customer service. In manufacturing, **production lines** and factories have become less labour-intensive with the introduction of automation, and more **capital-intensive**.

**labour supply or working population**   Those members of a country's population willing and able to work (*see* **labour**). It includes those currently in employment and self-employment, and also those who are registered as unemployed. It will exclude those in full-time education above the age of 16, those below the age of 16, those above retirement age, and those who have taken early retirement. It will also exclude those who choose not to work, the largest group of which are married women, and those unable to work because of illness or disability. As well as changes in the overall level of population, labour supply is also influenced by social factors. An increasing number of married women now seek employment; a growing number of young people continue their full-time education beyond 16; and early retirement for both men and women is also becoming more popular.

**labour turnover**   The rate at which the **labour** force leaves a business. It is measured by dividing the total number of workers leaving in a year by the total number in the workforce. For a business, a high labour turnover will lead to high **costs** in the **training** and **recruitment** of the new workers, and might be an indication of poor worker morale and poor wages. A low labour turnover will show a more loyal and perhaps better motivated workforce, and will help keep administration costs down.

**land**   The natural resource which forms one of the **factors of production**. This includes both the physical land (and sea bed) belonging to a country, and also the natural resources that are found in the land, such as oil and minerals. The distribution of land between countries is obviously fixed as land cannot be moved geographically, although land can be 'mobile' in terms of its use, e.g. agricultural land can be converted to housing or industrial use. The payment made for the use of land is known as **rent**, which is the reward for bringing land into use.

**lateral merger**    The joining together of two firms at the same stage of production which produce similar, but not identical products, for example, a chocolate manufacturer and a biscuit manufacturer.

**leadership**    An attribute required of anyone in charge of a group of people, or who represents a particular group within a larger organization. Good leadership may involve an individual having certain traits, e.g. intelligence, initiative, self-assurance, energy, etc. However, leadership also depends upon the nature of the group and individuals being led, and the nature of the task the group is facing.

The style of leadership adopted will depend upon the nature of those competing needs. **Autocratic leadership**, where the leader makes decisions without discussion, might be appropriate where quick decisions are needed and where the groups are not well motivated. **Democratic leadership**, where decisions are discussed, might be needed where the group and leader are on an equal footing and where a range of ideas is needed before a decision is taken. Thus the style of leadership required depends upon the situation in which decisions are being taken.

**lean production**   A production technique which originated in Japan and aims to employ the minimum of **inputs** in terms of employees, machines, buildings and materials. **Just-in-time (JIT)** is essential to lean production as this enables the business to hold a minimum level of stocks of raw materials and components thus keeping factory space to a minimum. The employees work as teams, so they need to be more skilled and responsible for their own **quality control**.

**leasing**   A method which businesses use to acquire the use of a **fixed asset** without incurring a large **capital** outlay. A business leases, for example, a machine or vehicle from its owners, and pays a rent for that asset, but the ownership of the asset does not pass to the business. The business has use of that asset until the lease expires, when it is returned to the owner. The leasing of company cars has become a common way for organizations to run a fleet of cars and update them at

regular intervals. The costs of maintenance and
**depreciation** of the cars are therefore not incurred by
the business but by the owners of the vehicles.

**legislation**   Laws made by the government which are
often referred to as 'Acts', for example, **Consumer
Protection Act**.

**liabilities**   What a business owes to those outside the
business. Liabilities are classified as either **long-term
liabilities** which are due for repayment after more than
one year, or **current liabilities** which are due within one
year. The type of liabilities that might be incurred by a
**public limited company** can be seen in the diagram
on the right.

**life cycle**   *See* **product life cycle**.

**limited company**   A type of business organization
which is owned by **shareholders**. The shareholders have
**limited liability**. There are two types of limited
company: a **private limited company** whose name
includes 'ltd', and a **public limited company**, recognized
by 'plc'. To start a private company there must be at
least one shareholder and one director. To start a public
company there must be at least two shareholders and
two directors and a minimum **authorized share capital**
of £50,000. There is no limit to the number of
shareholders for either company and both types must be
registered with the **Registrar of Companies**.

---

### Long-term Liabilities

**Debenture Loans**

**Bank Loans**

**Mortgage Loans**

**Unsecured Loans**

### Current Liabilities

**Trade Credit**

**Accrued Expenses**

**Bank Overdraft**

**Provisions for Taxation**

**Provisions for Dividends**

*liabilities*

Most private limited companies do not have to prepare and publish their accounts in the ways that a public limited company must, but private companies are not allowed to sell their shares on the open market.

**limited liability**    A situation where the owners of a company are only liable for the amount of **capital** that they have put into the company in the event of that company being wound up. This is applicable to the owners of **private** and **public limited companies,** and co-operatives. **Sole traders** and **partnerships** do not have limited liability. In effect this means that if a partnership was to run into large debts, the partners might be liable for the whole debt of the business, irrespective of how much capital they had put into it. Limited liability has allowed the expansion of businesses as **shareholders** will be less afraid to invest in a business when they know that there is a limit to the debts they might incur if the business closes down. *Compare* **unlimited liability**.

**liquidation**    The winding-up of a **limited company**, brought about by either the **shareholders** or **board of directors** (voluntary liquidation), or the **creditors**. Under liquidation, the **assets** of the company are sold, the debts repaid where possible, and any remaining money is distributed back to the shareholders.

**liquidity**    A measure of how well prepared a company is to repay its **current liabilities**, that is, its short-term debts. This will depend upon the level of **current assets** that the business holds in terms of stock, debtors and its balance at the bank, which can quickly be turned into **cash**. Liquidity is the speed at which an asset can be turned into cash for meeting bills and short-term debts. Cash is the most liquid asset; money due from debtors depends upon the time that people who owe money to the business take to repay, and stock depends on the time it takes to sell the goods being held in stock. Some of the stock might not be saleable, which will reduce the level of a company's liquidity.

When a business finds it difficult to repay its immediate debts, then it is facing a liquidity crisis. *See* **accounting ratio**.

**loan**    A general term for the borrowing of a sum of money by a person or organization from another person or organization. Loans might be for a short-term or a long-term period. A bank loan for anything less than about seven years is generally classed as a short-term loan. They might take the form of a secured loan, that is, one that is backed up by some form of collateral, for example a property. This would mean that if the loan is not repaid then the lender could take possession of the property. They might also be unsecured. The lender will charge an **interest rate** for the loan to cover the **opportunity cost** of not using the money in another way. The longer the loan is for, and the larger the organization borrowing, the lower the interest charged is likely to be. In business, loans are an important source of medium-term finance, especially from banks and other financial institutions.

**local agreement**    An agreement between local **trade unions** and local **management**, in which they may decide that they will alter a **national agreement** over **wages** and **working conditions** to take into account local factors. For example, local agreements in the London area may take into account the extra cost of housing in this area and pay a higher wage or **salary** rate than any national agreement. Local agreements should take into account the local conditions of supply and demand in the labour market (*see* **labour supply**). There has been a trend in recent years away from national agreements and bargaining towards local agreements and bargaining.

**lock-out**    A type of **industrial action** where the management prevents the workforce or a group of workers from coming to work on the existing terms and conditions. This has traditionally been done by locking the factory gates, and thus locking out the workforce. A lock-out might also occur after the sudden sacking of a group of workers. A lock-out is sometimes difficult to distinguish from a strike, because the lock-out might occur as a result of some industrial action the workers have taken. Lock-outs were common in 19th-century Britain, when other workers would be brought in at lower wages than those locked-out. In recent years there have been examples in the newspaper

industry, where employees have been locked-out for
wanting union recognition, or for refusing to operate
new machinery.

**logo**   A symbol or picture, often based on a **brand**
name or **trademark**, which is used by a company to help
**consumers** identify and remember their products, e.g. in
advertisements and on packaging. A successful logo
will help to increase customer awareness of a
product, and increase sales. The trademarks of
companies such as Shell and Coca-Cola are
internationally recognized, and are protected by their
owners against copying by competitors. Logos are an
important feature of the mass-marketing of consumer
products and services.

**long-term liability**   A debt owed by a business
to a person or individual outside the business which is
due to be repaid in more than one year's time. Common
types of long-term **liability** include debentures, which
are loans with a fixed interest rate and a set repayment
date purchased by individuals; bank loans, which are
often used for medium-term finance (2–5 years), and
**mortgages** raised for the purchase of land or factories.
The amount of long-term borrowing from outside the
firm, in relation to the firm's own **capital**, determines
the rate at which a business expands; the higher the

borrowing, the faster the potential for expansion, but also the greater the risk. *See also* **current liability**.

**loss leader** A product sold at a loss in order to attract customers into a store. This loss will be covered by the prices of other products in the store.

# M

**management**    The employees of an organization who are responsible for its day-to-day running. Managers carry out the decisions of the directors by organizing and coordinating resources, both human and physical. It is the role of management to plan the activities of the organization, motivate the workers and monitor progress. Managers may delegate some responsibilities.

**management buy-out**    The sale of a business by its owners to a group of managers of that business, who continue to manage the operation but also now have a share in the profits of a business. This has become a popular way to ensure the continuing independence of an organization under threat from closure or **takeover**, and has also been used by large organizations to allow them to sell off one part of their business. The managers have often had to arrange financial backing for a buy-out from banks or other financial institutions, as they would be unlikely to have sufficient funds as a group. Such finance is frequently forthcoming because the management have already shown their experience in running the business.

**managing director**    The person appointed by the **board of directors** to be responsible for the **management** team that runs a business. The managing director will also be a member of the board, and this will be important in passing policy decisions down to management and providing information from management to the board. He/she might have worked their way up through the company, or might have been appointed from outside. The managing director will be an employee of the company, possibly also owning shares in the company.

**marginal cost or contribution cost**    The extra cost a firm incurs when it produces one extra unit of output. This information can be used to analyse costs by a method known as *marginal costing*. This involves looking at those costs which will change as a result of a change in output of a particular product and separating them from

|  | **Product A** | **Product B** |
|---|---|---|
|  | £ | £ |
| **Sales Revenue** | 10,000 | 5,000 |
| **Less Marginal Costs** | 7,000 | 4,000 |
| **Contribution to** | | |
| **Overheads** | 3,000 | 1,000 |

|  | **Products A & B** |
|  | £ |
| **Total Contribution** | 4,000 |
| **Less Overheads** | 2,000 |
| **Profit** | 2,000 |

*marginal cost*

general overhead costs which will not change.
In the example above, by using a marginal costing
approach, the business can see the contribution that
each of its products is making to its overheads and
thereby to profit.

**market** A place where buyers and sellers exchange
**goods** or **services** in return for other goods and
services. Examples of types of market are shown in the
diagram overleaf.

**market research** The finding out of information to
help with the making of **marketing** decisions. This can
be done either by *desk research,* which is the collecting
together of existing data which has already been
collected and published for another purpose; or by *field
research,* which is the collection of original data for a

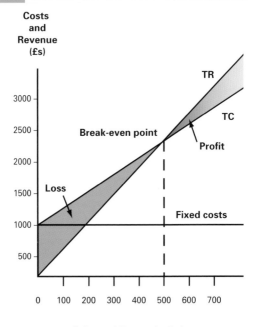

**market** *Types of market.*

specific purpose by carrying out a survey based on a structured questionnaire or interview of a sample of individuals in the population. Panels or groups of consumers might also be used as a basis for field research. Larger organizations will have their own market research department, but there are also many agencies which will carry out the research on behalf of the company. In carrying out market research, every organization must judge whether the cost of collecting the information is less than the benefit gained from using the information.

**market segment**    That part of a **market** consisting of **consumers** with similar characteristics. Ways in which a market might be segmented include age, income, socioeconomic grouping, sex, geographical location, 'lifestyle' of the consumer, the benefits which consumers feel they desire from the product, price. For example, a soap manufacturer might use age or sex as a way of segmenting a product, or might also use benefits like 'value for money' or 'freshness'. For the business, the advantage of using segments is that they can target their **marketing** campaign more accurately, perhaps identifying a 'gap' in the market for which a new product would be developed.

**market share**    A measure of the proportion of the total sales of a market that a particular product or brand holds. If, for example, the total market sales for some product were valued at £15m, and if company A had sales of £10m, company B £3m, company C £2m, then their market share would be as follows:

| | | **Market Share** |
|---|---|---|
| **Company A =** | $\dfrac{£10m \times 100}{£15m}$ | 66.7% |
| **Company B =** | $\dfrac{£3m \times 100}{£15m}$ | 20.0% |
| **Company C =** | $\dfrac{£2m \times 100}{£15m}$ | 13.3% |

Market share is often used as an indication for the success of a business – company A would be regarded as the market leader. A falling market share, even if the figure is still high, might suggest that a product needs a redesign or a new marketing campaign, or that a new competitive product is better than the existing products.

**marketing**   The identification or anticipation of customer **demand**, and the satisfaction of that demand by the development, **distribution** and exchange of **goods** and **services**. Marketing is now seen as the central function of many organizations which have developed a **market-orientated** approach to decision-making. As a function, it embraces a wide range of activities, including **market research**, **product development**, pricing, sales, promotion, distribution and after-sales service. The marketing department will have responsibility for these activities in larger organizations and plays an important role in company policy-making. *See also* **marketing mix**.

**marketing campaign or marketing strategy** The combination of promotion, **distribution** and pricing strategies that a company adopts over a period of time for a specific product. A concentrated campaign will be needed for the launch of a new product, for the relaunch of a product, or for launching into a new market or in reaction to a competitor's campaign. Often a campaign will involve a coordination of advertisements, posters, sales promotions and special offers. Usually such a campaign would be designed and organized by an **advertising agency**.

**marketing mix** The combination of **marketing** plans and policies that are employed by an organization in order to achieve its marketing objectives. In its simplest form, it can be represented by policies adopted in four areas, the **four Ps** (*see diagram*) but there can be a large variety of elements employed within each category.

The exact combination of such policies employed by an organization will depend upon the size and resources

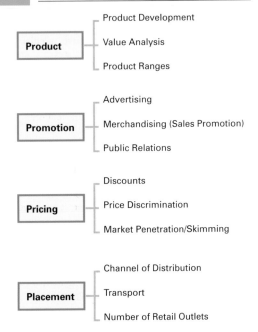

***marketing mix*** *The four 'Ps'. Some examples of policies used as part of the marketing mix.*

of the organization, the nature of the product, the nature of the market and the state of competition in the market. For example, larger breweries market lager by heavy expenditure in **advertising** and wide-scale **distribution** in public houses; smaller breweries rely on quality of product and lower prices, but will employ less advertising and use fewer outlets.

**market-orientated**    Directed towards the **demands** of the market. A market-orientated approach to developing a product is one which puts the desires of the **consumer**, as reflected in **market research**, at the centre of the decision about what to produce. This is often compared with a **product-orientated** approach, where a product is developed before it is established that there is a **market** for that product.

For most **consumer goods**, producers have become market-orientated because of growth in competition and the increasing knowledge of consumers about what is available. Products, such as cookers, cars, motorcycles and televisions, have to be attractive to the customer to sell against competitors as all the products now perform their basic functions in a similar way. Service industries like banking and insurance have also become more market-orientated, for example in the way student accounts are sold by banks (*see diagram overleaf*).

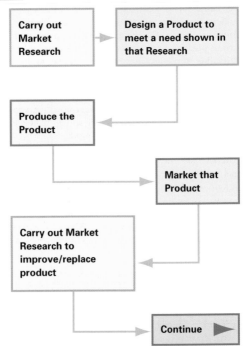

***market-orientated*** *Product development.*

**market-orientated pricing**    Methods of pricing which take into consideration the market conditions relating to the product. These will include competitors' prices, consumers' expectations, the firm's market share. *See also* **penetration pricing**, **price discrimination**.

**mark-up**    A method of **pricing** a product whereby the seller takes the basic **average cost** of the product and adds a fixed percentage constant to determine the price of the product. This will therefore allow the business to ensure a profit on each sale. Thus if product A costs £2.50 to produce, it might sell for £3.25, a 30% mark-up. Such a method of pricing is common in the retail industry, where a shop will add a fixed percentage mark-up (e.g. 100%) on the purchase costs of **stock** in order to cover the selling costs and **overheads** of the retailer. Such a method of pricing does not really take into account the state of the **market**, although discounts will be offered to attract more customers if the market situation demands it.

**Maslow, Abraham (1908–1970)**    An American psychologist who developed the model shown overleaf to help explain how people are motivated (*see* **motivation**). This model is known as the *hierarchy of needs* and is shaped like a pyramid.

According to Maslow, people seek to have their *physical needs* such as warmth, food and shelter satisfied first. Once these are satisfied they then want their *security needs* satisfied, e.g. a home, a family, safety. At the next level are the *social needs* of love, being part of a group, a sense of belonging, and then the *ego needs* of doing work, being congratulated, being successful and at the top, *self-fulfilment needs,* i.e. a sense of achievement, responsibility and personal growth.

Once a need is satisfied, it no longer motivates, and people look towards the next higher need. If a need is not satisfied, then it can lead to frustration and aggression.

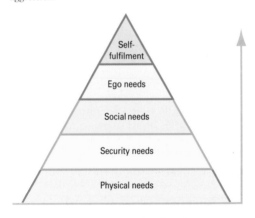

**Maslow** *Hierarchy of needs.*

**Mayo, George Elton (1880–1949)** The founder of the human relations school of management, who carried out a series of investigations at the Hawthorne Plant of the Western Electric Co. in Chicago, between 1927–32. In the first investigation he looked at the way different working conditions such as different hours of work or rest periods affected the work of a group. He found that the changing conditions were less important than the social effects in the group of having the researchers studying their activities. Thus employee attitude to work was seen as more important than the work itself.

In a second investigation, he discovered the importance of groups in determining the output of a department: groups set their own targets, and ignored targets or incentives given by the management. The investigations showed that employees should not be thought of as just motivated by money and good conditions, as was held by the followers of **Taylor**, but that the nature of the job, of supervision, and of the working group were also important factors. *See* **informal organizations**, **McGregor**.

**McGregor, Douglas (1906–1964)** A supporter of the human relations school of management, who devised two contrasting sets of ideas about what motivated people in organizations, Theory X and Theory Y.

## Theory X

- Average worker is lazy.
- He/she lacks ambition, dislikes responsibility, wants to be led.
- He/she is self-centred and not interested in the organization.
- He/she is resistant to changes.
- He/she is motivated by money.

## Theory Y

- People are not lazy and passive – they are made to be so by experience.
- They have the capacity to accept responsibility, to lead, to accept organizational goals.
- They can get motivation from their job and the people around them.

McGregor saw a Theory X manager as organizing production, directing people, controlling, persuading, rewarding and punishing the workforce to get things done. He saw a Theory Y manager as trying to create an opportunity for workers to develop their own responsibility and also to achieve their own goals within the organization's objectives. McGregor himself favoured the Theory Y approach, and supported the idea of **job enrichment** so that the workforce could achieve a higher **motivation**. *See also* **Mayo**, **Taylor**.

**media**   *See* **advertising media**.

**Memorandum of Association**   One of the documents that the owners of a company have to place with the **Registrar of Companies** when the company is formed. It contains the name of the business, the type of business it is, the address where the company is registered, the name of those people providing the capital for the company and the number of shares they own, the amount of share capital that is to be raised, and the **limited liability** nature of the company. This information will help to protect the interests of future investors or customers of the company. It is deposited along with the **Articles of Association**.

**merchandising**   That aspect of **marketing** that tries to pull the **consumer** to a specific product. The process is aimed at a specific group of customers, perhaps those within a shop,  and often lasts for a limited period of time. Included under this heading will be such factors as point-of-sale promotions, price reductions, free gifts, special offers, competitions and special events. The term is also used to cover the packaging and production of goods which are also designed with promotion in mind. *See also* **advertising** and **marketing mix**.

**merchant banks**    Banks that provide a number of specialist financial services for other businesses. These include the provision of **loans**, the management of **investments**, dealing in foreign currency, and the acceptance of bills of exchange. They provide an important source of **venture capital** for new business projects and advice and assistance for small businesses. They also help to arrange share issues and play a leading role in the organization of **mergers** and **takeovers**. They are also known as investment banks.

**merchantable quality**    Under the **Sale and Supply of Goods Act (1994)**, all **goods** sold by a business must be fit for sale, i.e. they should be fit for the purpose for which they are bought. For example, if a pair of shoes are purchased and the heel falls off on the first wearing, then they are not of merchantable quality. But it is not always clear what fit for sale means: e.g., how long should new shoes last? A refund can be claimed if the goods are not of merchantable quality, and damages in court can also be claimed if any accident occurs. Two exceptions are (a) where the **consumer** examines the goods before they are bought, (b) where the seller points out any fault that exists before the sale takes place. The idea of merchantable quality is one of the oldest types of consumer protection that exists.

**merger**    The joining together of two firms. This might be (a) because one business has taken over another, i.e. has bought enough shares in that business to gain a controlling interest, or (b) because the two firms have agreed to join together. Mergers can be of a variety of types.

If a secondary producer merges with a business at the same level of production and produces the same product this is a **horizontal merger**. If the two businesses produce similar goods, then this is called a **lateral merger**.

If a secondary producer merges with a primary producer, then this is a *backward* **vertical merger**. If a secondary producer merges with a tertiary business which distributes its goods, this is a *forward* vertical merger. If two businesses in totally unrelated businesses merge, this is a **conglomerate merger**.

Horizontal mergers are often arranged to increase the **market share** and power of a business, and to allow greater **economies of scale** to occur. Lateral mergers allow an increased range of goods to be produced. Vertical mergers are arranged to ensure a guaranteed source of supply or a guaranteed outlet for a product. Conglomerate mergers are often completed to increase the profitability of a business for the benefit of shareholders, or to spread the risks of being in one industry only.

**merit goods**   These are **goods** and **services** provided by the government for everybody, because if the provision was left to the private free market they would not be provided at the right price in the right quantity. Such goods include state education, health care, and the social services. Most modern societies subscribe to the principle that such services should be available to everyone, irrespective of whether they would wish or be able to consume them. Such goods are often provided free of charge or at a low price, and are paid for out of taxation collected from everyone.

**minimum wage**   The lowest legal limit for **wages**. The British government, in line with the National Minimum Wage Act (1998), sets a national minimum wage for all workers. In addition, some industries set their own wage scales. The limit might represent the statutory wage for a new entrant on the bottom grade of the industry. The wages would probably be set above the level that might be earned through social security payments for workers who are unemployed. Minimum wages are often negotiated to prevent exploitation of workers by **management**, and to ensure that every worker has a minimum standard of living. **Trade unions** are often in favour of minimum wage agreements. Some economists oppose the concept of general minimum wage on the grounds that it might prevent some employers from deciding to take on extra workers, and therefore create **unemployment**.

**mixed economy**   An economy, such as the UK, where some decisions about production are made by the

**private sector**, and some are made by the **public sector**. It has characteristics of both a **free market economy** and a **planned economy**. The majority of health care is in the public sector, while retailing is a private-sector industry. The majority of Western and developed economies are mixed economies, although they vary considerably in their mix. For example, the public sector in France is larger than in the UK; the private sector in the US is larger than in the UK. A free market economy is one where all decisions are made by the private sector, but this does not exist in real life. A planned economy is one where the government or state makes all decisions. The former Soviet Union and China used to try to be planned economies but, this too, is difficult.

**modern apprenticeship**  *See* **apprenticeship**.

**monetary policy**  One of the major economic policies that a government can employ. It involves the control by the government or its central bank of the availability of money (**money supply**) or the cost of money (the **interest rate**). If the government wishes to control inflation it might seek to reduce the level of **demand** in an economy, so will reduce the rate of growth of the money supply and/or increase the rate of interest, i.e. the cost of borrowing money. This will make **consumers** and businesses less willing and able to borrow money to buy **goods** and **services** or investment goods. If the government wishes to reduce unemployment, it might seek to increase the level of demand in an economy, so will increase the rate of growth of the money supply and reduce the level of interest rates, which will encourage borrowing and spending.

**money supply**    The amount of money that is in existence in an economy at any one time. Money takes a variety of forms, and therefore the money supply can be made up of a number of elements. These include notes and coins in circulation, **current accounts** in banks and building societies, and **deposit accounts** held in a variety of financial institutions. The rate of growth in the money supply on a monthly basis is an important economic statistic which governments use to indicate the levels of activity in the economy. Control over the rate of growth in the money supply was seen by one group of economists as a major way of reducing excess demand in an economy and thus **inflation**. Others argue that the **interest rate** is a more important tool for controlling demand than the level of the money supply.

**Monopolies and Mergers Commission (MMC)**
A body set up by the UK government in 1948 which, when directed by the **Office of Fair Trading**, will examine a business or industry to see if it is using its **monopoly** power against the public interest. It will also investigate mergers between businesses which might

lead to a monopoly (**horizontal merger**) and any anticompetitive activities by a business or group of businesses. In the UK, a monopoly can exist where one firm has over 25% of the market for a **good** or **service** in a national or local context. The MMC can recommend that (a) a **merger** should not take place, (b) a monopoly should be reduced, or (c) a **restrictive practice** should be abandoned if they find that such developments are against the public interest. Each case will be treated on its merits.

**monopoly**   A **market** situation in which one firm has at least 25% control over production and pricing, and in which other firms are prevented from competing by barriers to entry. The monopolist is therefore able to charge whatever price it wishes and restrict its output when necessary. This behaviour will ensure maximum profits for the firm, but will be against the interests of the **consumer**. It is rare for pure monopoly to exist in practice, as **competition** from alternative products often occurs. *See also,* **Monopolies and Mergers Commission (MMC)**, **restrictive practices**.

**mortgage**   A type of finance used by individuals and agencies to purchase property. A **loan** is made by a building society, bank or insurance company, covering a proportion of the purchase price of that property to be paid back over a set period of time (often 25 years).

The institutions making that loan retain ownership of the property as security for the loan until the loan is repaid.

**motivation**     The reason, or incentive, for doing something. It is especially important when assessing the reasons why people work. Researchers like **Taylor** argued that money and **working conditions** are the most important motivators. The human relations management school see social needs, self-esteem, a sense of achievement and an opportunity to be involved, as more important in motivating people at work. An owner or manager of a business needs to be aware of ways of motivating individuals at work; the leadership style adopted by a manager will often determine the opportunities for motivation that exist in a job for an individual. *See* **job enrichment**.

**multinational corporations**     A company which is based in one country but also operates to a substantial degree in a number of other countries where it owns and operates factories or outlets for its products. The company can therefore take decisions on an international scale, and is not easily controlled by the rules or economy of any one country. Thus it might decide to close down a factory in country A where **wages** are high, and open a factory in country B where wages are low. For the company, the benefits of being multinational include the freedom to concentrate resources where they will earn the best return. However, individual countries and regions might suffer from the decisions of multinationals which are based outside their shores. Groupings of countries such as the **European Union** find it easier to regulate the behaviour of multinationals than individual countries.

# N

**national agreement**   An agreement between national **trade unions** and national employers' federations which determines the basic **wage** structure and **working conditions** for an industry. Thus the Engineers' Union (AUEW) will negotiate with the Engineering Employers' Federation to reach a national agreement for the engineering industry. There might also be a national agreement in a large public company between the company **management** and national trade union representatives. There is now a move away from national agreements towards local pay bargaining and **local agreements**.

**National Vocational Qualification (NVQ)**   A qualification which assesses competence in skills related to a specific vocational area, for example Business Administration, Distribution or Information Technology. Modern **apprenticeships** will lead to at least NVQ level 3, and **Choices Training** can lead to NVQ levels 1, 2 or 3.

**nationalized industries**   These are industries which are owned and run by the government, which form part of the **public sector**. Set up by an Act of Parliament, policy is decided by a minister of the government, but day-to-day management is left to a chairman of the board. Electricity, coal, the railways, gas, the Post Office and iron and steel, have all been under public ownership in the UK at some time since 1945; but under the policies of **privatization** introduced in the 1980s, several, including gas, telecommunications and steel, have been returned to the **private sector**. Arguments for having nationalized industries include: control over essential industries, the prevention of **monopoly** power, protection of the public interest and financial support from the state. Arguments against have concentrated upon the lack of **competition**, the lack of efficiency and the size of their bureaucracy.

**needs**   The **goods** and **services** which are considered to be essential for survival. These basic needs are identified as food and drink, clothing and shelter. Goods and services which are not necessary for survival are referred to as **wants**, for example TV sets, fashion clothes and holidays. Work helps to satisfy needs; **Maslow** recognized that we have different levels of need, from the basic ones of survival, food and shelter, to the higher ones of love, respect, status, recognition and achievement. While having a job can help to satisfy the lower needs, work for many has been less able to satisfy the higher needs, which might explain many people's dissatisfaction with their jobs.

**negotiations** Discussions between two or more people aimed at reaching an agreement that is acceptable to both sides. In **industrial relations**, it is common for representatives of **management** to meet with representatives of the employees (often **trade unions**) to negotiate over **wages** and other conditions of employment, in a process known as **collective bargaining**. If negotiations break down the two parties are often referred to **ACAS**.

**net pay** The amount of money an employee receives after deductions have been made for income tax, national insurance, and for various voluntary contributions. These might include a fee for **trade union** membership, a contribution to a pension scheme, a contribution to a save-as-you-earn scheme, or a donation to a charity. Therefore the net pay will be lower than the **gross pay**; and is often called *take-home pay* or disposable income, as it represents the amount that the employee actually receives.

**net profit** This is the amount of **sales revenue** that a business earns, less all the costs involved in achieving that revenue, including both **direct costs** and expenses (*see diagram on the right*). The net profit figure represents the figure for profit before taxation or dividends are further deducted, and shows how successful a business has been in generating profits from its trading activities. *Compare* **gross profit**.

## Company X Profit-and-Loss Account 2002

|  | £ | £ |
|---|---|---|
| Sales revenue |  | 1,000 |
| less cost of goods sold |  | 350 |
| GROSS PROFIT |  | 650 |
| less overheads and expenses: |  |  |
| Salaries | 100 |  |
| Rent, rates | 80 |  |
| Misc. expenses | 70 |  |
| Depreciation | 80 | 330 |
| NET PROFIT |  | 320 |

**New Issues Market**    One of the markets that make up the **Stock Exchange**, this is the market which deals with the raising of new long-term **capital**. Those organizations which wish to raise long-term capital offer shares for sale to the public, to other businesses, and to financial institutions on this market.

There are a number of alternative ways of raising long-term capital. Shares might be issued directly to the public by way of a prospectus, or through an issuing house such as a **merchant bank** which will underwrite the issue in case insufficient people wish to buy the new shares. Shares might be privately placed with large investors before any general issue. Existing companies might also raise money from existing **shareholders** by a rights issue whereby, at a discounted rate, more shares are issued to existing shareholders.

**no-strike agreements**    The **trade union** agrees not to strike but if any dispute arises which is not solved through **negotiation,** both the management and the trade union agree to accept the decision of an independent arbitrator. This is an example of the 'new style' agreements which are a feature of the changing attitudes of trade unions and are intended to promote closer co-operation between management and trade unions. Another example is the **single-union agreement**.

**nonprofit-making organizations**    Any of the organizations, such as those often found in the

voluntary sector of an economy, whose major objectives
are other than to achieve a **profit** for distribution to their
owners or investors. Charities such as Oxfam or the
British Legion are good examples, where money raised
from their trading activities is used to fund charitable
activities in the UK and overseas. Their aim is to
generate as much income as possible in order to use as
large a percentage as possible to help those in need.
Many public-sector organizations will also be
nonprofit-making, for example libraries, museums, social
services and healthcare organizations.

**nontariff barriers**   In trade with other countries,
these are the factors which prevent **free trade**,
and which are not the result of a tax on **imports**
(*compare* **tariff**). Such barriers might include a physical
**quota** in the amount of goods being imported, or a
physical ban or embargo on trade. Concern has also
been expressed about other types of barrier which
might distort trade, for example different **indirect tax**
systems, different levels of domestic subsidy, different
laws, rules and regulations covering businesses, and
different quality standards. Nontariff barriers have
caused problems in the **European Union** where tariffs
between members have been eliminated. In 1992, the
EU removed many nontariff barriers between the
member nations.

**NVQ**   *See* **National Vocational Qualification**.

# O

**objective**   The particular goal that an organization is
trying to achieve. It is increasingly recognized that, to be
successful, any organization must have a clear view of
what it is trying to achieve, i.e. its objectives. A range of
possible objectives has been identified for different
aspects of business. For a small business, survival or
growth might be appropriate objectives, while the
maximization of **profits** might be important for the
owners of a larger business. For a management team in a
competitive market, sales maximization, or having a
certain **market share**, might be important, while for a
**public-sector** organization, a good service to the public
might be the objective in view. Objectives are also
important in that they provide a measure against which
the performance of an organization can be compared. In
a similar way, individuals at work are increasingly set
objectives in their jobs to help to motivate and to
evaluate their performance. *See* **motivation**.

**Office of Fair Trading**   A UK government
department set up in 1973, under the Director-General
of Fair Trading, to protect the interests of the **consumer**
in relation to trading activities. The Office oversees the
workings of the **Monopolies and Mergers Commission**
and the investigation of any restrictive trade practices by

businesses. It also has responsibility for ensuring that good trade practices are followed by businesses, and that law-breakers change their methods of selling. *See* **Fair Trading Act (1973)**.

**official receiver**   An official of the UK Department of Trade and Industry who takes charge of the affairs of an individual or company which has been declared bankrupt or insolvent. The receiver will help to realise the **assets** of the **debtor** (i.e. sell them) and distribute the proceeds amongst the **creditors** where possible, with each creditor receiving a percentage of what is owed to them.

**official strike**   A strike by a group of employees that has the backing of the **trade union** that represents those employees. This means that the dispute between **management** and employees has been given official recognition by the latter's trade union officials at regional or national level. An official strike cannot occur until a secret ballot of the workforce likely to be involved has been carried out. Most national strikes are official, whereas most local strikes are unofficial. Official strikes tend to be more widespread and longer-lasting than **unofficial strikes**, but are much less likely to occur than unofficial ones. They usually occur because of a breakdown in negotiations over pay and conditions at a national level.

**off-the-job training**    The process of learning skills and attitudes about a job when employed, but where the learning takes place off the premises of the employer. Such training mainly takes place in colleges of further education, but also in institutes of higher education, technical colleges, universities and specialist training or management centres. Traditionally, such training has been thought most appropriate for professional, technical and managerial staff, but training for supervisory and skilled workers is now increasingly including an off-the-job element, while such schemes as **Choices Training** involve a period of college-based work. With the increasing need in modern society for trained workers to be more flexible and to be able to transfer between jobs, the need for wide-ranging off-the-job training has increased. *Compare* **on-the-job training**.

**on-the-job training**    The process of learning job skills at the place of work. Most introductory, inductive-type courses for new employees will be based at the employer's premises, and the majority of training for unskilled and semiskilled workers will be based on 'hands-on' experience at the workplace. In addition, apprenticeships for skilled crafts have traditionally been based on the idea that the trainee learns directly from a skilled worker on-the-job. However, many apprenticeships now include a period of general **off-the-job training**, while government-approved training courses such as **Choices Training** include both on-and off-the-job training. Businesses will therefore carefully consider the costs of running their own on-the-job training schemes, which have the advantage of giving direct control over how their employees are trained.

**opportunity cost**   The benefit that could have been gained from an alternative use of the same resource. (All economic decisions involve an element of choice as there are limited resources to satisfy unlimited wants.) For example, if a business decided to spend £100,000 on a new machine that will generate a 15% return on its investment, the opportunity cost might be the lost interest on that money if it had been left in a bank deposit account. In a similar way, if the funds were left in the bank, this opportunity cost could be the returns from other uses which are not being achieved while the money is in the bank.

**ordinary shares or equities**   Those shares which give the **shareholder** a part-ownership of the company in which they have invested. They form the largest single source of long-term **capital** for companies. Ordinary shareholders can vote on how the company is run. This depends on the numbers of shares that are owned, as one share carries one vote. If the company makes a profit, and if the **board of directors** so decides, the ordinary shareholder will receive a share of the profit in the form of a **dividend**. This will vary according to the size of the company's **profit** and the amount of that profit which the directors decide they wish to plough back into the company. Dividends for ordinary shares are distributed after interest for **debentures** and dividends for **preference shares** are deducted. If no profits are made, or only a very low level of profit, the ordinary shareholders may receive no dividend. However, liability for debts is limited to the amount that each individual shareholder has invested in the company. Once issued, ordinary shares for **public limited companies** can be bought or sold on the **Stock Exchange**.

**organization chart**    A diagram (right) which is used to represent the formal relationships within an organization. These relationships are designed to achieve the objectives of that organization. The organization chart for a medium-sized brewery might look like the chart shown. This chart takes the form of a **hierarchy**, but charts are now produced which are circular or box (matrix) shaped, to reflect different types of organization.

**output**    The **goods** and **services** produced by a business. Output is a flow, measured over a period of time, and therefore would not include items already produced but held in stock. Where output is difficult to measure, as in a service industry, then the number of customers or value of sales might be used as a measure

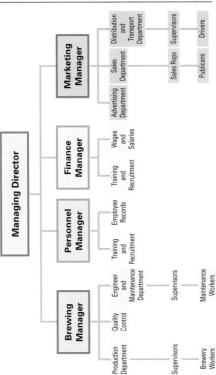

***organization chart*** *A hierarchy within a brewery.*

of output. Output, when compared with an element of a firm's inputs (*see* **factors of production**), such as number of employees, or level of **assets** employed, can be used as a measure of how efficient the firm is in comparison with other firms and other time periods. When the output of a whole country is calculated, this is known as the Gross National Product.

**overdraft**    An excess of cash allowed by a bank to a business or personal customer, permitting the withdrawal of more funds from a **current account** than are there, up to a certain limit. The customer pays interest on the amount that is actually overdrawn at any one time, rather than the whole amount of the **loan**. This makes an overdraft a flexible and relatively inexpensive source of short-term funds for a business to meet uncertain day-to-day cost requirements. However, interest charged on overdrafts is higher than the interest on longer-term loans, so if a business expects to be overdrawn for a period of time, a bank loan would be a better source of finance. A bank might also require an overdraft to be repaid immediately, as there is no agreed time limit for this type of loan. Managing the overdraft is an important part of the management of a business's **cash flow**.

**overheads**    Those **costs** of a business that cannot be allocated to a particular cost centre, product or section.

They are usually divided into *factory overheads, selling and distribution overheads, administration overheads* and *financial overheads.* As businesses have to be able to meet these costs as well as those which can be directly allocated, various methods are used to try to allocate them in a scientific way. For example, selling overheads might be allocated between products according to the level of sales of each product, factory overheads might be allocated by the factory space that each product takes up. Any method used, because of the nature of overheads, will only be an arbitrary way of allocating those costs. *See* **direct costs**, **indirect costs**.

**overtime**  The period of time worked by employees over and above what is agreed to be a standard working week in their contract of employment. The employee is likely to receive a rate of pay for overtime that is greater than their normal hourly rate; time-and-a-half or double-time pay is common. In many industries in the UK, a considerable amount of overtime is worked, and for many workers on low basic pay, overtime pay is seen as an important way of boosting the final weekly or monthly pay packet. For **management**, it can be useful to help meet production deadlines or sudden rush orders. However, the existence of overtime might prevent higher productivity during working hours. *See* **overtime ban**, **Working Time Regulations (1998)**.

**overtime ban**   A type of **industrial action** where employees stop short of **strike** action, but refuse to work any hours beyond their normal contracted hours. Because **overtime** is common in many industries, such a ban can have a considerable effect on the output of a firm or its ability to provide a full service. From the employees' point of view, they would not be in breach of contract for carrying out such a ban, and are thus less likely to be dismissed by employers. In industries which operate for 24 hours a day, overtime bans can severely disrupt production or services, and can be just as effective a means of industrial action as a strike.

# P

**packaging**  The purpose of packaging is to protect the product, attract customers' attention and display a description of what the package contains. Packaging is an aspect of **promotion** which is aimed at persuading the customer to choose the firm's product rather than that of a competitor.

**partnership**  A type of legal organization for a business which has the following features. There can be between two and twenty owners. All partners are legally responsible for any of the firm's activities as the firm does not have a separate legal existence. Each partner also has **unlimited liability**, meaning that all partners are liable for the debts of the business. There is usually also a partnership agreement which states how the business is to be run between the partners, how much **capital** each has put in, and how the **profits** will be shared. Partnerships often end on the death of one of the partners. Partnerships are common among professionals such as doctors, solicitors and architects, where the advantages of the increased finance that partners bring and the increased possibility of sharing out the work are very important.

**patent**  An agreement made by the state that an inventor of a new industrial or commercial process is given a **monopoly** over its use for a given period of time. In the UK, the patent is registered with the Patent Office, where it is checked to make sure that it is new, that it involves an 'inventive' step, and that it is capable of industrial application. A patent will last for 20 years if it is granted, and will protect the inventor from other individuals or firms stealing the invention. If an employee invents a process as part of his or her normal job, then it is considered to belong to the employer, although the inventor should receive compensation.

**pay**    The reward for **labour** providing its service, usually comprising either a weekly **wage** or a monthly **salary**. Pay is seen as one of the most important forces in motivating the workforce (*see* **motivation**), but is also one of the major causes of dispute between **management** and workforce. It is also recognized that nonfinancial rewards are becoming more important for employees, and that pay is not the only motivating force within a job. From the **gross pay** of employees, income tax and national insurance contributions are deducted to give **net pay**.

**payments system**    A method of organizing the payment of employees. There are many different ways of paying groups of workers, including **time rate**, **piece rate** and **bonus payment** systems. Many organizations have a number of grades or scales for the different types

and level of employee, and for each grade a different
type of payment system might be employed. Most
payment systems include a ladder of payments to allow
for experience and promotion, and to encourage the
workforce to stay within the organization rather than
seek higher pay elsewhere.

**penetration pricing**   A low price set initially to
enable a firm to gain a foothold in a new market. This is
often used when new products are launched. Prices can
be raised at a later date once the new product has
become established.

**performance related pay (PRP)**   A **payments
system** for motivating **white-collar** and **service**
workers who are not directly involved in production or
sales. It is a scheme which links the employee's
**salary** to their standard of work, or performance. The
employee will be set targets or given specific duties
which will be reviewed periodically. Rewards will
depend upon the degree of success the employee
has shown in meeting targets or in carrying out their
specific duties.

**person specification**   A description of the ideal
person for the job. It identifies the qualifications, skills,
experience and personal qualities required. These are
often classed as 'essential' and 'desirable'.

**personal selling**   The **promotion** of a product through the direct contact between the seller and the customer. Sales staff will inform the customer about the product through demonstrations and discussion, and persuade the customer to buy the product by offering advice, **after sales service** and personal attention. Personal selling is carried out by sales assistants in retail outlets, 'door-to-door' sales representatives and telephone selling.

**personnel department**   The department within a firm (often called 'human resources') that is responsible for relations between employer and employee, and for the employee's general welfare. The diagram shows the personnel department's responsibilities.

As organizations have become more concerned about the welfare and motivation of their workforce, so the importance and scope of the personnel department has increased, and specialists have been employed to make up the department. It might also concern itself with **communications** within the organization, and with how the organization itself is structured.

**picketing**   A way of furthering a **strike** or other form of **industrial action** by placing people outside the place of work involved in the dispute to present their arguments to anyone who wishes to enter that factory, office or site, in the hope of dissuading them from entering. There are considerable legal controls over

**personnel department**
*The department's main responsibilities.*

picketing, but peaceful picketing as part of a trade dispute is legal. However, pickets are not allowed to physically intimidate anyone going about their legal duty, nor is secondary picketing allowed at the place of work, i.e. pickets from another area who are not already involved in the dispute, or pickets from a business which is not itself in dispute with the workforce.

**piece rate**    A system of payment whereby a person (or group, if appropriate) is rewarded according to **output**, i.e. how much he or she produces. For example, a farmworker picking strawberries might receive £1 for every 5lbs of strawberries picked. Thus the more strawberries the worker picks, the higher will be the pay he or she receives, and there will be an incentive for the workers to increase their productivity to increase their pay. A disadvantage of this method of payment is that there may be a need for more **quality control**.
Piece rate payment is becoming less common as it is recognized that a **basic pay** level should be set irrespective of how much is produced, and that pay is only one factor in providing **motivation** for the workforce. It has also become more difficult to identify who produces what in an automated production line. *See also* **commission**.

**place**    The element of the **marketing mix** which refers to the **distribution** of goods.

**planned economy**  A type of economic organization where the **factors of production** are owned by the state, and where decisions about what to produce and how to produce are also made by a central agency. Thus resources are allocated by decisions made by a central administration. Plans are made to take into account the likely production needed by each sector of the economy to meet its desired objectives for the economy in terms of consumption, investment, growth, etc. Such a system is seen as fairer than a **free market economy**, as income will be distributed more fairly, and may make it easier for the economy to reach certain targets. However, planned economies have found it difficult to be efficient; there are few incentives for the workforce, and the planning itself requires a large bureaucracy to operate. The economies of the former Soviet Union, China and other communist countries have been centrally planned ones, but most such economies have now allowed more free-market elements to operate legally. The UK is a **mixed economy**.

**preference share**  A type of **equity** which gives the holder a part-ownership of a business, but unlike **ordinary shares** pays a fixed **dividend** rather than a variable one. The preference **shareholder** has priority over ordinary shareholders when the profits are shared out, and if the company goes into **liquidation**. However, because the risk involved in holding preference shares is less, the return is also likely to be less. It may be that in some years a business will not pay any dividend to ordinary or preference shareholders, although cumulative preference shares enable the holder to receive any lost dividend in later years when the business is more profitable.

**pressure group**    An organization which exists to influence public opinion about a particular issue, with the hope that local or national government will change their policies to achieve the objectives of the pressure group. Pressure groups usually want to make something happen or prevent something happening. They are not political parties, but may hope to influence the policies of these parties. **Trade unions**, the **Consumers' Association** and the Friends of the Earth are all examples. Businesses might need to take heed of pressure groups if the latter succeed in changing the legal basis for business activity, or if they affect the public image of a business or industry by a particular campaign. Businesses themselves, however, form pressure groups to try to influence policy in favour of a group of businesses. For example, the **Confederation of British Industry (CBI)** attempts to influence the government to choose policies favourable to industry.

**price**    The element of the **marketing mix** which refers to **pricing policies**, price is the **market** value of **goods** and **services** that are bought by **consumers** and firms.

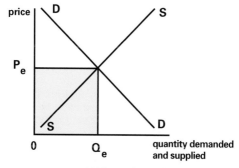

***price*** *(a) The market settles at $P_e$.*

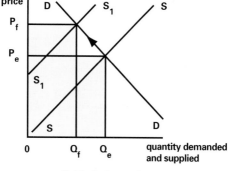

***price*** *(b) The higher market price is at $P_f$.*

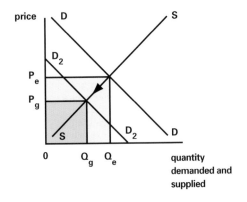

***price*** *(c) The lower market price is at P<sub>g.</sub>*

Prices act as the information system which allows
markets to operate. In a **market**, the price of a good or
service is determined by how much the supplier is
willing and able to supply, matched against how much
the consumer is willing and able to buy.

In diagram (a) the market will settle at $P_e$, where the
amount consumers are willing to buy is just matched by
the amount producers are willing to supply. If **costs**
were to rise or if consumer wishes about the product

were to change, then the price would change to bring a
new market equilibrium. Thus in diagram (b), where
costs of production have risen, the new market price
will be higher at $P_f$. In diagram (c), where the tastes of
consumers have moved away from the product, the new
market price will be lower at $P_g$.

**price discrimination**   The charging of different
prices to different **market segments** in order to
maximize **sales revenue**. Hairdressers, for example, may
charge lower prices to old-age pensioners and children,
to attract customers. Price discrimination is sometimes
refered to as *differential pricing*.

**price elasticity**   The responsiveness of a **demand** for a
product or service to changes in the price of that
product. It can be measured by using the following
formula:

$$\text{Price Elasticity of Demand} = \frac{\text{Percentage Change in Quantity Demanded}}{\text{Percentage Change in Price}}$$

For **goods** and **services** where the elasticity is greater
than 1, demand is *elastic,* so a small change in price will
result in a large change in demand. Where the elasticity

is less than 1, demand is *inelastic,* and even a large change in price will not cause demand to change by very much. It is expected that necessities will have a lower price elasticity than luxury products, and that goods with close substitutes will have a lower elasticity than those without close substitutes. Businesses will find the concept useful in order to judge the likely effect of a price increase or decrease on their sales level and on their sales earnings. If demand for their product is price elastic, then a price cut would be a favourable strategy to increase earnings. If demand is price inelastic, then a price rise would be a favourable strategy.

**price plateau**  The **price** which a customer expects to pay. If the price is too high then the customer might refuse to buy the product, but if it is too low the customer could think that the good is inferior.

**pricing policy**  The overall policy pursued by a firm in pricing its products. The price that a business decides to charge for a product will depend upon a range of factors: (a) the costs of **production** and how it chooses to allocate those costs to specific products, (b) the type of **market** in which the business is operating; (c) the type of product that the business is selling – whether it is a new one or already established, whether it is a high quality one, (d) the behaviour of competitors – whether price is the normal form of competition and (e) the pricing strategy that the business wishes to employ, linked to other elements of the **marketing mix**, e.g. does the company start with a low price to gain a large market share quickly (**penetration pricing**) or with a high price to ensure a high profit margin straight away (**skimming**)? *See also* **price discrimination, price plateau.**

**primary data**    Information collected through **market research** for a specific purpose. Unlike **secondary data,** it is collected first-hand by field research methods, i.e. surveys and questionnaires.

**primary production**    The stage of economic activity that involves the extraction of natural resources from the land so that they can be used in the secondary stage of production. Therefore the extraction of oil, gas, coal and other minerals would be classified as primary production as well as the production of food crops and animal products by farms. Extraction from the sea such as fishing would also be included. In developed economies, the level of primary production only forms a small part of total production and the number employed in the primary sector is also small. But in less developed countries, primary production forms a greater part of economic activity, in terms of both output and employment. *Compare* **secondary production, tertiary production.**

**private benefits**    The gain an individual consumer or business receives from a business activity, for example, the opening of a health club near a housing estate. A private benefit to a consumer might be the convenience of having the facility near to his home; a private benefit for the business would be the profits from running the health club. These benefits can be either financial, i.e. the profits the business gains, or non-financial, i.e. the convenience the consumer gains. *Compare* **private costs, social benefits, social costs**.

**private costs**    The loss, or negative effect, which an individual consumer or business experiences as a result of a **business activity** such as the opening of a health club near a housing estate. A private cost to a consumer might be the annual subscription which must be paid for using the health club (a financial cost). The private cost for the business could be the time and effort needed to launch the business and make it a success (a non-financial cost). *Compare* **private benefits, social benefits, social costs**.

**private limited company**    A **limited company** that does not issue **shares** for public subscription, and whose owners do not enjoy an unrestricted right to transfer their shareholdings.

**private sector**    That part of a **mixed economy** in which decisions about what to produce, how to produce

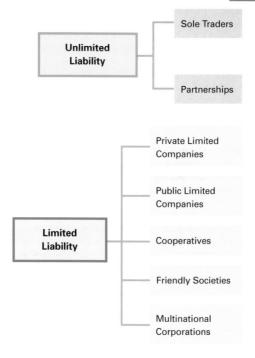

***private sector*** *The UK private sector.*

and where to produce are made by private individuals based on free market information provided by the price system. In the UK, the organizations in the diagram on page 171 make up the private sector.

**privatization**    The process of government transference of a business or industry from the **public sector** to the **private sector**. It does this by offering shares in the business to the public in a flotation on the **Stock Exchange**. Previously, the shares of the business would have been owned by the government. In the UK there have been a number of large share issues to privatize industries, including British Airways, British Telecom, British Steel, British Gas, National Power and Powergen. Arguments in favour of privatization suggest that it would increase competition, improve efficiency and reduce government expenditure and hence the level of taxation. Arguments against suggest that the government is needed to protect the public interest, that national assets are being sold to private individuals, and that many of the newly privatized companies can act freely as **monopolists** to raise **prices** and lower the quantity and quality of **services** for the public, beyond government control.

**producer goods**    Those items produced by a country which are purchased by other businesses rather than **consumers**. This would include **capital goods** such as raw materials, factory buildings, tools and machinery and those **consumer goods** which are also bought for businesses, for example, cars for sales people or managers, stationery for offices, food for canteens.

**product development** The process of a business bringing new products into the **market**, or adapting and improving upon existing products. There are three major strategies that an organization might choose. It can carry over its own **research and development** to develop its own products, it can use existing research to develop new products, or it can take products that have already been developed (perhaps by competitors) and adapt them for a particular market. The major stages of product development will involve searching for new product ideas, examining the likely viability of each idea from a commercial viewpoint; making the product, testing that product on the market, and finally a full scale product launch. At each stage, decisions have to be made about whether the product is likely to be successful; most products do not survive the development stage.

**product life cycle** A model of how the sales of a typical product might behave over the life of that product (*see diagram overleaf*).

The model suggests that during introduction, sales will be low, but following a successful launch the rate

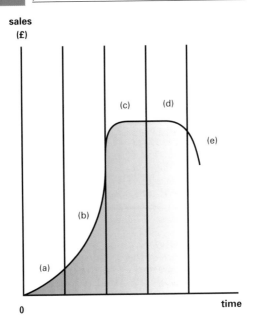

**sales (£)**

(c)

(d)

(e)

(b)

(a)

**time**

0

**product life cycle**  *The different stages represent (a) development, (b) growth, (c) maturity, (d) saturation, (e) decline.*

of sales will increase quickly (growth). During maturity, sales will steady at a high level, until the market reaches a saturation point. From then, the sales may go into decline.

For a business, this model shows that it needs to be aware of the possible future decline of successful products. It might introduce some new marketing strategies to extend its product's life, and might also make sure that there are new products in development to replace mature and declining products. *See* **product-orientated**.

**product mix**    The variety of different products a business will produce at any one time. To maintain a steady level of **sales revenue**, there should be a balance between products in different stages of their **product life cycle**.

**product-orientated**    Directed towards the product and its efficiency. In a product-orientated business, the nature of the product itself, its features and technical strengths, form the most important element in the development, production and selling of that product.

For many companies which produce machinery, tools or other **producer goods**, the product and its specifications will be the most important element in the business's decision-making. In most **consumer good** industries, their production has become **market-orientated**, i.e.

### Primary production

The extraction of raw materials from the earth and sea, e.g. mining, farming.

### Secondary production

The manufacturing of products such as clothing or cars from raw materials or other manufactured products.

### Tertiary production

The provision of services which help to allow primary and secondary production to occur and which help distribution of products to consumers. These services can be personal, e.g. teaching, health care, or commercial, e.g. transport, banking.

*production*

what the market wants comes before the technical efficiency of the product. *See* **product life cycle**.

**product range**   The different design of a basic product which will attract different market segments. A company will produce a range of cars to satisfy customers' different tastes and income.

**production**   The process by which an organization transforms raw materials, using financial and human resources, into an end product that is consumed by someone else. Production activity can be classified into three stages, as shown in the diagram on the left.

   Each organization at each stage of production helps to add value to the resources that are used as they are transformed into new products and services. The total value of all production in an economy in a year is its Gross National Product. For methods of production, *see* **batch production**, **flow production**, **job production**.

**production line**   A method of organizing machinery and labour in **flow production**, where the parts of a product pass directly from one operation to another without stopping until the final product is produced. The motorcar assembly line is an example of such a production line. Machinery and tools have to be lined up to allow for continuous assembly, and each worker or group of workers is given a small task to complete before the product moves on to the next operation.

Quite often the product will keep moving throughout the line. Although the process involves high **fixed costs**, the **average costs** will be low once production is continuous. For the workforce, the work might well be repetitive and arduous, and the amount of skill required is low. Many production lines have become automated to remove the need for workers to do repetitive jobs. *See also* **job enrichment**, **quality control**.

**productivity**     A measure used by businesses for the level of **output** in relation to the use of **factors of production** such as **labour** and **capital,** i.e. the rate of production. *Labour productivity* is calculated by comparing the level of output with the number of worker hours employed, while *capital productivity* compares output with the level of capital employed. Productivity is important because it measures efficiency; a low level of productivity by one firm in comparison with another might suggest that improvements in their operations would be needed. Increasing productivity would mean falling **average costs** of production and should allow increased profitability in a business.

**productivity bonus**     A **bonus payment** given as a reward to employees for achieving an output target.

**profit**     What is left when all **costs** incurred in making and selling a product are deducted from the revenue gained from that sale. It acts as the reward to the

**entrepreneur**, usually the owner of the business, who has provided the capital. It is usually the **net profit** after tax which represents the surplus for the owners of the business and is paid as a **dividend** to **shareholders**.

Profit maximization is seen as one of the major objectives of a business, although it is more likely to be an objective for the investors in a business, than for its managers or employees. It might be for those groups that profit acts as a constraint, while higher sales or higher wages and salaries are more important objectives.

**profitability ratio**   *See* **accounting ratio**.

**profit-and-loss account**   One of the two final accounts that a business prepares, that shows how much **profit** or loss the business has made through its trading and nontrading activities over a given period of time.

The profit-and-loss account is divided into three parts: the **trading account**, which shows the **costs** and revenue resulting from its trading activities; the profit/loss account which shows revenue earned and costs incurred outside its normal trading activities; and the *appropriation account*, which shows what is done with any profit earned.

A published profit-and-loss account for a **public limited company** would be as shown overleaf.

The figure for retained profit could also appear as part of the **shareholders' fund** in the **balance sheet**.

| | £ | |
|---|---|---|
| **Sales revenue** | 100,000 | |
| Less: costs of goods sold | <u>50,000</u> | Trading Account |
| **Trading profit** | 50,000 | |
| Non-operating income | <u>5,000</u> | |
| Profit Before interest & tax | 55,000 | Profit/Loss Account |
| Less: interest | <u>15,000</u> | |
| Profit before tax | 40,000 | |
| Less: tax | <u>15,000</u> | |
| Profit after tax | 25,000 | |
| Less: ordinary dividends | <u>5,000</u> | Appropriation Account |
| Retained profit for that period | 20,000 | |

*profit-and-loss account*

**profit maximization**   It is assumed that all businesses will want to make as much profit as possible, and that this is their main **objective**. However, a business might have an alternative objective, for example, just to survive, or to grow as big as possible, or to gain the biggest market share.

**profit-sharing**   A scheme whereby employees are given, as part of their payment, a share in the **profits** that they have helped to generate. Profit-sharing has become more common in UK companies in recent years. This acts as a bonus on top of the normal wages or salary. In some organizations, as an alternative, employees are encouraged to become **shareholders** in the company, and therefore they receive a share of the profits through the **dividends** paid. Arguments for profit-sharing are to (a) reward employees for their work in generating the profits; (b) involve the workforce in the success and running of the enterprise; (c) provide an incentive to encourage the employees to work harder as they will have a share in the profits. Problems can arise if the firm makes a loss, and if workers owning shares wish to leave the business.

**promotion**   As one of the **four Ps**, promotion seeks to inform and persuade consumers to buy products. Promotional activities include **advertising**, **sales promotion**, **public relations**, **personal selling** and **packaging**.

**provision**   A sum charged against a firm's **profits** in anticipation of **costs** that are likely to arise in the future. A company will make a provision when it expects to pay a certain sum in the near future and so records this as a **current liability** on its **balance sheet**, but until the sum is paid it can make use of the money as a short-term source of finance. The amount that a business has to pay in tax will be known in advance and so provisions for taxation will appear, as will provisions for **dividends** to be paid. Until the tax and the dividends are paid, the money set aside may be used on a short-term basis to increase the business's **working capital**. In a similar way, a business might make provisions for future losses, e.g. provisions for **bad debts**, if they know that they will occur. This will involve a deduction from the **profit-and-loss account**, treating the bad debt as a cost, and as a reduction in the level of **debtors** on the balance sheet.

**psychological pricing**   A price which is set to encourage customers to believe that they are gaining an advantage, for example, charging £9.99 instead of £10.

**Public Interest Disclosure Act (1998)**   An Act that offers protection to employees who disclose information, in the public interest, about certain types of wrongful activities by their employers. It is sometimes referred to as the Whistleblowers' Act. It allows people to raise concerns about alleged criminal or civil offences, miscarriages of justice, or danger to the health and safety of the public or the environment, without jeopardizing their jobs.

**public limited company (plc)**   A form of **limited company** where the public are invited to buy **shares,** and so become owners of the business through the issue of those shares on the **Stock Exchange**. Thus, while two people are the minimum needed to set up a plc, there is no maximum number of owners, and many large plcs have thousands of **shareholders**. This helps provide the companies with a large financial base, and plcs are the largest of the **private sector** organizations. Each shareholder has **limited liability**, and each share owned gives them a vote in the overall running of the business. Directors are elected by shareholders to represent their interests, while the directors appoint managers to make the day-to-day decisions on running the company. The majority of well-known UK companies are plcs, including BP, ICI, Sainsburys and National Westminster Bank. Since the government in the UK has been following a policy of privatization, a number of new plcs have been created, e.g. British Gas, British Telecom, and British Aerospace. *See* **limited company**.

**public organization**   An organization established and owned by the government, and under the control of governors appointed by the government. The day-to-day decisions, however, will be made by a management team, appointed by the governors, but otherwise able to run the corporation with a degree of independence. Public corporations form a part of the **public sector**; all **nationalized industries** come under this heading, as do organizations such as the **Bank of England**, the BBC and IBA, the Atomic Energy Commission and the Forestry Commission. They are set up by Act of Parliament, and the objectives are expressed in terms of public service, i.e. protecting the interests of the public rather than the objectives of the **private sector**. However, with control by governments over public expenditure, public corporations are now given limits on how much they can borrow from the government, and have had to operate following commercial objectives to keep within these limits.

**public relations (PR)**    A department found in larger organizations which is responsible for communications between the organizations and those people in the outside world who come into contact with the organization, for example customers, suppliers, **shareholders**, employees and politicians. Through public relations, an organization tries to promote a good image for itself, and to influence people to think favourably about the organization and its products. One way that this is achieved is to ensure favourable comments and information about the organization in newspapers and on radio and TV. Within the organization, staff journals and newsletters might be another way of improving public relations. A good public image helps with **promotion**. *See also* **marketing mix**.

**public sector**   That part of a **mixed economy** where decisions about what to produce, how to produce and where to produce, are made by a central authority rather than left to private individuals and the workings of a **free market** (*compare* **private sector**). Resources are owned by the state, and are allocated in a way to ensure that all individuals are best served, rather than following the interests of one group. The public sector is made up of central and local government departments, and public corporations such as the **nationalized industries**.

In recent years, through its policy of **privatization**, the UK government has reduced the size of the public sector by transferring some nationalized industries, and responsibilities for some public services, into private hands. *See also* **planned economy**.

**purchasing**   An important function in organizations, dealing with the purchase of the materials necessary to allow the **goods** or **services** of that organization to be produced. For a manufacturing company, purchasing will be responsible for buying a large range of raw materials, components and parts, but even in a service organization, purchasing will need to buy in office equipment, stationery, etc., and other services such as canteen facilities, security and cleaning. In purchasing, the organization will try to ensure quality at the best value for money, and will often be able to negotiate **discounts** for bulk buying. However, a business will not want to hold too high levels of stock, and so purchasing needs to monitor the rate of usage, and balance this with new purchases.

# Q

**quality circle** A small group of workers who meet regularly to discuss problems related to quality, efficiency and work in general. The idea originated in Japan and it aims to develop teamwork and improve **motivation** as well as solving problems. *See also* **quality control**, **job enrichment**.

**quality control** Businesses have increasingly recognized the importance of quality if their product or service is to satisfy the needs of customers. Quality control concerns the methods businesses use to make sure that the product will meet the standards expected by the customer. When products are inspected during production it may be sufficient to inspect one sample. However, some customers, e.g. Marks and Spencer, will insist on 100% inspection because they have built their reputation on high quality. Businesses tend to encourage a quality approach in the whole organization to make sure that the product's quality is not let down by any part of the organization. An organization will need to be aware of the costs of quality control, including reject costs, inspections and testing costs, balanced against the costs of not having good quality control, i.e. goods returned, repairs under guarantee and poor product image. *See also* **job enrichment**, **quality circle**.

**quota**    A restriction on the amount of a product that can be imported into a country over a certain period of time. In a similar way to **tariffs**, their aim is to restrict the level of **imports** and therefore help improve a country's **balance of payments** and protect its domestic producers. Quotas are usually imposed on a certain product rather than on a country; for example, the **European Union** has quotas imposed on the number of cars that can be imported from outside the member countries each year. As well as restricting volume, quotas are likely to cause the prices of the restricted products to rise.

**quota sampling**    A method of **sampling** used in **market research** where groups of people who share certain characteristics are chosen to be interviewed. For example, an interviewer might be asked to interview a certain number of males between the ages of 18-25, or females between 45-60. The groups should be proportionate in size to their representation in the population as a whole.

# R

**racial discrimination**   The unfavourable treatment of an employee or potential employee because of his or her race. Under the UK Race Relations Act (1976), it is illegal for an employer to treat a person 'less favourably' on grounds of race than other persons in similar circumstances in their job, in recruitment for the job, in promotion to other jobs, in their pay and conditions, or in dismissal. It is also illegal to advertise for workers in such a way as to create discrimination. If an employee finds that he/she has been discriminated against, the case can go to an **industrial tribunal**, and the Commission for Racial Equality may also take the employer to court to prevent further discrimination.

**random sampling**   A method of **sampling** used in **market research** where every interviewee has an equal chance of being chosen. Stratified random sampling is more representative than random sampling. The population is divided into segments, e.g. males, aged 18-25, and then random sampling is used within the 'segment' or 'stratum'.

**rate of stock turnover**   An **accounting ratio** which represents the speed at which a business sells its products. It is calculated on the following lines:

---

**Cost of Goods Sold**

---

**Average Stock at Cost Price**

---

A high number means that the stock is fast moving, e.g. in a supermarket, whereas a low number indicates slow moving stock.

**recruitment**    The process of obtaining a supply of new workers to enter an organization, which is usually the responsibility of a **personnel department** in larger organizations. Methods of recruitment will differ depending upon the type of person being recruited. For young recruits, schools, colleges, universities, careers officers and training schemes will provide the main source, while for older recruits, job centres, employment agencies, trade unions, families and other businesses will be important. The process of recruitment involves establishing a **job description** and **person specification**, designing a means of advertising the vacancy, sifting through the applications received, interviewing a number of the applicants, making a selection and reviewing the progress of new recruits. Some organizations employ outside agencies to recruit staff for them, especially for managerial jobs.

**redundancy** The situation that results when an employee's contract of employment is ended because that job no longer exists or is no longer needed. A factory might close down, which would make all the workforce redundant, or, within a factory, a new machine might make a particular job no longer necessary. Workers who are made redundant have a right to receive compensation in the form of a lump-sum payment which varies according to the length of service of the employee. Many companies in fact negotiate with **trade unions** to give more than the minimum legal requirement in compensation, especially if they are asking for workers to accept voluntary redundancy as opposed to compulsory redundancy. Disputes about redundancy levels and payments can result in industrial disputes between workers and **management**.

**regional selective assistance** *See* **Assisted Areas**.

**Registrar of Companies** The government official who is responsible for recording details of companies established in the UK.

**rent** The reward paid to the owners of **land** as a **factor of production** used in economic activity. Thus, the rent paid for offices and the rent paid for factories are the prices that a business is paying to the owners of those offices or factories for use of those buildings on their land. Rent is also the term used to describe the price paid for the hiring of any durable good, such as a copying machine or a telephone. To a business, rent is an **overhead** cost which must be met out of the revenue of the business. Because land, offices, etc. are immobile in the geographical sense as factors of production, rents in areas such as London where land is scarce, are likely to be very high because of competing uses and high demand.

**research and development (R&D)**   The use by an organization of part of its resources to investigate and experiment with new products or process developments, with a view to introducing them at a later date into the organization. Such a development will be expensive to run, but the rewards will emerge in improved future performance by the organization. The risk to a business from expenditure on R&D is that competitors might not devote time and expenditure to such resources, but might still be able to copy any new developments. For smaller organizations, separate R&D departments will be too costly; sometimes they group together to share the costs of R&D across the whole industry, with part of the funding coming from each company. *See also* **product development**.

**restrictive practices**   Those practices that occur where companies in the same trade work together to avoid **competition**, often at the expense of the **consumer** or other businesses. For example, businesses might collude, to agree to keep prices high or restrict output to push prices up. It is felt that, just as with **monopolies**, such practices discourage competition, encourage inefficiency, and discourage innovation. Since 1973, the Director-General of Fair Trading has been responsible for overseeing restrictive practices.

**Retail Price Index (RPI)**    A measure commonly used to indicate the rate of **inflation** in an economy. The index shows the average price rise or fall in **goods** and **services** sold in shops over a period of time, using 100 as the base figure. For example, if retail prices between 1996 and 1997 rose by 8% on average, then if 1996 was the base year, the index for 1997 would be 108. The RPI is calculated by comparing the prices of a 'basket' of goods and services, purchased from a range of retail outlets, from one month to another, with each price change weighted according to the relative importance of that good or service in a family budget. As a measure for inflation it is important for businesses because it often forms the basis for employees' wage and salary increases and for government policy.

**retailing**    The last stage in the **channel of distribution** which involves the final selling of the **goods** and **services** that have been produced to **consumers**. The function of retailing is to provide the consumer with a local supply of goods in small quantities. Types of retailer include door-to-door, mail order, market traders, independent shops, retail **cooperatives**, chain stores, supermarkets, department stores, and hypermarkets. The retailers will cover their **costs** and gain a profit margin by adding a percentage to the cost price of the goods traded to obtain the retail price. This is the retailers' **mark-up**. Within retailing, the trend has been towards larger shops, sometimes located in shopping areas outside the town centre, and more multiple chains with shops throughout the country with the same name and merchandise. **Franchising** has also grown in importance, often allowing the creation of chains of smaller shops.

**retained profit**    The amount of **profit** after tax that directors of a business decide not to distribute to their **shareholders**, but to keep within the business. It is held as an increase in the **capital** and reserves of the business, and will be used to expand the operation of the business through the purchase of **assets**. The retained profit will be 'ploughed' back into the business in the form of increased fixed assets, or increased current assets – usually only a small proportion will be held as a cash reserve. Retained profits form the most important source of finance for business expansion in the UK. *Compare* **distributed profit**.

**rights issue**   A way for **public limited companies** to raise extra finance by offering their existing **shareholders** 'rights' to buy new shares in the business. This might be, for example, on a one-for-one basis. To make this offer attractive, the extra shares are offered at a discount below the existing market price of the shares, with the hope that once the issue is taken up the market price of the new shares will be considerably higher than their issue price. Plcs would use rights issues because they offer a much cheaper way of raising capital on the **Stock Exchange** than the high costs of a new issue of shares.

**risk**   All business decisions involve an element of risk, because there are a number of possible outcomes from a decision. Often, businesses will try to calculate the amount of risk attached to each alternative outcome, by using probabilities which are based on previous experience or forecasts. For example, in considering the launch of a new product, the business might estimate that there is a 25% probability of a successful launch and a 75% probability of a failed launch. These probabilities will be weighed against expected **costs** and **profits**, and will be used to compare the launch of a new product with other alternatives. An **entrepreneur** takes risks.

**risk capital**   *See* **venture capital**.

**risk management**   All firms face **risk** and they try to make an allowance for this when making decisions. Risk management involves strategic decision-making, often using statistical techniques, which will result in the highest possible profit for the minimum level of risk.

# S

**salary** A type of payment to an employee where a certain sum is negotiated on an annual basis and paid in monthly parts. Salaries are the common form of payment among white-collar workers in professional, managerial and scientific employment. Because such jobs do not produce a specific **output**, nor might they fit into a specific period of hours, a salary is a more appropriate method of payment. However, within their contract, most salaried workers will be required to attend work for an agreed minimum number of hours and to carry out a certain number of duties. *See also* **wages**.

**Sale and Supply of Goods Act (1994)** This law combines the Sale of Goods Act (1979) and the Supply of Goods and Services Act (1982) and extends consumer protection by requiring that all goods and services must be of satisfactory quality, which provides for situations which existing laws do not specifically cover. For example, a washing machine which rusts after six months could meet all the requirements of the Sale of Goods Act (1979), but under the updated Act, the consumer could claim a refund or replacement as it is not of 'satisfactory quality'. The act maintains the requirements of the Sale of Goods Act (1979), which requires that goods must be:

- **Of merchantable quality, i.e. the goods should be of reasonable quality, not broken or faulty, e.g. a watch must not keep stopping,**

- **As described, which means they must match the description given by the seller or on the packaging, e.g. a watch described as having a leather strap must not have a plastic strap,**

- **Fit for the purpose for which they have been bought, e.g. a watch must keep the time accurately and run neither fast nor slow.**

These requirements are extended to services under the Supply of Goods and Services Act (1982). For example, repairs and servicing, hiring and leasing are covered. All services should be carried out in a reasonable length of time, to a reasonable standard and for a reasonable price.

**sales bonus**    A **bonus payment** where an additional payment is made to sales staff on top of the basic pay

based on the number of sales made over a period of
time. **Commission** is a type of sales bonus.

**sales promotion**    A *below-the-line* method of
persuading customers to buy goods. It is generally aimed
at increasing sales in the short term. Examples of sales
promotion include money-off coupons, competitions,
free offers and free samples. Sales promotions can also
involve celebrities endorsing the product, or charity-
linked promotions where every purchase means a
standard contribution will be made to a specific charity.

**sales revenue**    The income that a business receives
as a result of selling its products. It is calculated in the
following way, over a fixed period of time:

$$\textbf{Sales Revenue = Price x Quantity Sold}$$

Sales revenue is the starting point for the calculation of
**profit** in a business with the costs being deducted from
the sales revenue (*see* **profit-and-loss account**). Changes
in sales revenue might occur due to changes in the price
of the product or changes in the volume of sales. An
increase in price will lead to an increase in sales revenue
if there is **price elasticity** in demand for the product,
and a decrease in sales revenue if demand is inelastic.
For a price cut, revenue will fall if demand is

price-inelastic, revenue will rise if demand is price-elastic. Other factors will also influence the level of sales revenue, such as changes in marketing policy, changes in competitors' behaviour and changes in the economic environment.

**sales turnover**    *See* **sales revenue**.

**sampling**    The testing of a small, representative quantity. Because it is often impossible or very expensive for an organization to survey all the members of a target population, it is necessary for only a small proportion of that population to be surveyed, known as a 'sample'. If the sample is large enough and chosen at random, then the results will, within known limitations, reflect the whole population. Sampling is most commonly employed in **market research** and in **quality control** where to survey the whole population or test all products would be expensive and time-consuming. The most common types of sampling are shown in the figure on the right.

**seasonal demand**    The variations in the level of purchase of a product by **consumers** according to the time of year. **Sales revenue** would therefore be much higher for a business at one time in the year than at another. The demand for holiday accommodation, for

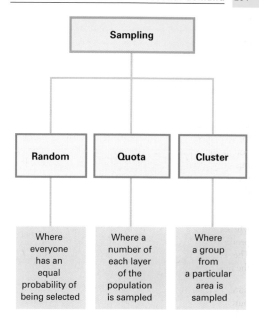

***sampling*** *some types of sampling*

ice cream, for greetings cards and for flowers would all demonstrate a number of fluctuations at different times of the year which are likely to be repeated each year. For businesses in such markets, low levels of income in certain months might lead to **cash flow** problems as costs will continue to be incurred. These might be avoided by developing products in different markets with different seasonal peaks. For example, hotels try to attract business people and conferences during the winter months when the tourist trade is low.

**secondary data**     This is existing information which has been gathered from previous research and investigations. Such investigations include marketing reports, such as those conducted by Mintel, government statistics, such as Social Trends, trade reports published by the CBI or TUC. Secondary data is collected by desk research methods. Desk research involves a researcher reading through information which has been collected for a different purpose and selecting what is relevant to their investigation. *See* **primary data**.

**secondary production**     The stage of economic activity where raw materials are transformed into semifinished or finished **goods**. This includes the manufacturing and construction industries. Although still an important activity in developed economies, its importance has declined in relation to the tertiary sector as these economies develop. Increasing **competition** has also come from newly industrialized economies such as Korea, Singapore, Taiwan and Hong Kong. *Compare* **primary production**, **tertiary production**.

**services**    Intangible, nonphysical products produced for households. They are usually consumed at the time of purchase, although for some services such as a holiday, consumers may be asked to pay in advance. Examples include commercial services such as **distribution**, **communication**, financial and professional services, and public services, which are those provided collectively by the government, e.g. health care, education, the police service and social services. Such services might be provided free of charge but paid for out of taxation. Those organizations which provide services are included in the tertiary sector of the economy. *See* **tertiary production**.

**sex discrimination**    The unfavourable treatment of an employee or potential employee because of their sex. Under the Sex Discrimination Act (1975, revised 1986) it is illegal for employers to discriminate against people on the grounds of sex or marital status. This would cover the advertising of jobs, recruitment, training, promotion or dismissal. The question of discrimination in pay is covered by the **Equal Pay Act**. Individuals who feel that they have been discriminated against can appeal to an **industrial tribunal**, where they can gain redress and compensation. The **Equal Opportunities Commission**

exists to oversee the legislation and to make sure that employers adopt fair employment policies.

**share capital** The money contributed by **shareholders** to a business which stays in the business as long as it exists and usually forms the **capital** which helps to establish the business. It may take the form of **ordinary shares** and **preference shares**. The shares of a **public limited company** may be bought and sold on the **Stock Exchange**, but they will continue in existence for as long as the business exists. *See* **authorized share capital**.

**shareholder** Someone who has a part-ownership of a company by holding a number of shares in return for providing some **capital** for the company. **Ordinary shares** will provide the holder with voting rights at the company's **annual general meeting** and therefore some control over the company's affairs. The interests of shareholders are looked after by the **board of directors**, as most individual shareholders have too few shares to be able to influence decisions. In return for providing capital for the business, shareholders will receive a share of the profits of the business, in the form of a dividend. They might also receive a capital gain on their investment if the price of their shares on the **Stock Exchange** rises.

**shift work** A method of organizing work when **goods** or **services** are to be produced over more than an individual's working day during the 24-hour period. This will involve employing more than one group of workers, known as a *shift,* who take over the tasks from the previous group at a specified time. If an organization runs two 8-hour shifts then these might be from 7 am to 3 pm and from 3 pm to 11 pm. Three shifts would cover the whole 24 hours. Work on a night shift may be paid for at a higher rate than that on a day shift. Shift work is likely to occur in mass-production industries where the machinery needs to be kept in continuous use, or where a 24-hour service needs to be provided, as in a hospital. Maintenance and cleaning work is often carried out in early morning or late night shifts.

**shop steward**　An employee of a business who also represents the interests of a group of **trade union** members in negotiation with **management**. Shop stewards are elected to their position and act as the union representative on the shop floor. They receive some paid time off to carry out their duties which include collecting union dues, giving out information from the union, passing on complaints to the management, and investigating individual **grievances** against management. Because they are the elected representatives of the workforce, they play an important role in negotiations at a shop-floor level between unions and employers. They might also organize official or unofficial **industrial action** if negotiations break down.

**single market**  *See* **free trade**, **nontariff barriers**.

**single-union agreement**  An agreement between management and employees that only one **trade union** will operate within the organization. This avoids the need for separate negotiations with several unions, thus saving time and avoiding constant uncertainty. The union acts like an **industrial union**.

**skimming**  A **pricing policy** where initially a high price will be charged for a new product so that the firm will be able to recover costs quickly from the **sales revenue**. Eventually the price will be lowered in order to interest more **consumers**.

**social benefits**  All the benefits that are gained by society as a result of a **business activity**. For example, a decision by a retailer to build a new supermarket on the edge of a town will bring increased benefits to society such as an increase in the number employed in the area, better shopping facilities, and lower prices as a result of more **competition**. *Compare* **social costs**.
*See also* **cost benefit analysis**, **private benefit**.

**social capital**  *See* **capital goods**.

**Social Chapter**  Section of the Maastricht Treaty of the EC covering labour and employment law. It deals with such areas as safety in the workplace, improvements in working conditions, rights to collective bargaining, equal rights for men and women, vocational training, remuneration and social protection. Although the British Government initially opted out of the clause, the newly elected Labour Government signed up in 1997. This led to a series of Acts bringing British law in line with the EC.

**social costs** All the **costs** that are incurred by society as a result of a **business activity**. For example, a decision by a retailer to build a new supermarket on the edge of a town will result in costs to society such as a loss of farming land, increased road traffic to and from the shop, and a loss of trade for shopkeepers in the town centre. *Compare* **social benefits**. *See also* **cost benefit analysis**, **private costs**.

**sole trader** A type of business organization where one person is the owner and where that person has sole responsibility for the decisions in the business. There is **unlimited liability**, which means that the owner will gain all the **profits** from the business but is responsible for all the debts of the business. There is no legal difference between the owner and the business. As the business is personal to the owner, it ceases to exist on the death of the owner. Finance for a sole trader usually comes from the individual's own savings or from family and friends. Therefore such a business is likely to stay small unless it expands to a **partnership** or **limited company**.

**span of control** The range of people within an organization for whom one person is directly responsible. In the example, the marketing manager has a span of control of four. Such a span shows that the senior manager has delegated responsibility for certain areas of operation to individuals lower down the organization. The size of the span in any situation will depend upon the nature of the work being carried out, the abilities of those in the span and the willingness of the person in charge to delegate. For example, someone supervising a group of workers carrying out very similar jobs might have a much wider span of control than the manager shown below.

*span of control*

**spreadsheet**   A software package used on personal computers for the presentation and calculation of numerate data. A spreadsheet is a matrix of columns and rows into which can be inserted headings, numbers or formulae. The program can then act as a fast calculator to present a completed set of figures and to recalculate all the related data quickly if there is a change in any of the data. A common business application would be in the preparation of accounting information, for example a set of profit-and-loss accounts or a **cash flow forecast**. Because the spreadsheet will recalculate the outcomes for each set of values that are entered once it is set up, it allows the user to ask 'what if?' type questions and to investigate their outcomes, a useful tool in forecasting.

**stock**   Materials or product kept by businesses. There are three types of stock: raw materials, work-in-progress and finished items. Stocks of raw materials or other supplies are kept to allow production to continue without delays and to take advantage of any bulk-buying discounts that exist. Items that are being processed will also be included as stock and are useful if delays in output at one stage of production occur. Stocks of finished goods act as a buffer in case there is a sudden increase in demand, and reduce the risk of late delivery.

**stock control**    The process of trying to establish the best level of **stocks** to hold. An organization has to balance the **cost** of holding stock, against the costs of not holding stock. The costs of holding stock include the **opportunity cost** of tied-up resources, the cost of warehousing, insurance and so on, as well as the costs of deterioration or of the stock going out of date. The costs of not holding stock include the loss of sales and customers, the possible disruption to production if stocks run out, and the loss of any discounts that might be available for bulk purchases. Such factors will determine the *maximum* and *minimum* levels of stock that an organization decides upon. But the exact nature of the stock-control system and the *re-order level* will depend upon the rate of usage of the stock, how frequently new stock can be brought in, and the *lead* time, i.e. the time it might take for the order to arrive. *See also* **just-in-time (JIT)**.

**Stock Exchange**    A **market** for long-term **capital**, where both new capital can be raised by companies and where existing shares can also be bought and sold. By providing a second-hand market for investors to sell their shares it facilitates the raising of new capital on the new issues market. The Stock Exchange also provides a market for government **loans** and securities, and is increasingly involved in the buying and selling of shares in overseas companies. On the market, the main operators are the market-makers who trade in a group of shares, and the stockbrokers who act as agents for their clients, who are the investors who are actually buying and selling shares. The Financial Times Share Index, an average of price movements in a number of important shares, is used as a guide as to how the Stock Exchange is performing, and sometimes as a rough indicator of the state of the economy.

In the late 1980s, the way the Stock Exchange operated was transformed by deregulation – the 'Big Bang'. This brought in **competition** over the fixing of commissions by brokers and market-makers, allowed outside institutions to take over the dealing firms, and brought more efficiency to the trading of shares. New technology was also introduced to speed up trading and help establish a worldwide market.

**strike**   The withdrawal of **labour**. It is the last resort that a group of employees can take if they feel that their demands or **grievances** about their work are unlikely to be met or redressed. A strike occurs when **collective bargaining** breaks down. The right to strike is regarded as a basic freedom in a democratic society. Traditionally, this was a right mainly exercised by manual workers, but strike activity is now more broadly based, with white-collar workers like teachers and civil servants showing a willingness to take **industrial action**. However, the vast majority of the workforce will not be involved in any strike action in any one year. A strike has an immediate effect on a business of lost output, but this loss might be made up when production starts again, so that the cost of a strike to a business is difficult to calculate. Alternatives to strike action, such as an **overtime ban** or a **work-to-rule** might in fact cause more damage to a company than an all-out strike because it might last over a longer period of time and the effects might be less predictable for customers. *See also* **lock-out**, **official strike**, **unofficial strike**, **industrial action**.

**subsidy**    A form of negative **taxation** where the government pays a sum to a producer to enable that producer to sell a product at a lower price than the **market** would normally allow. The producer is therefore subsidized to produce more of a product at a certain price than their **costs** would allow. The customers will benefit through either lower prices or more plentiful supplies. Subsidies have been most often used in agriculture, where the government has been attempting to keep the price of food down.

**supply**    The amount of a **good** or **service** at a given price that producers are willing to bring onto a **market**. The figure shows a supply curve and suggests that, as the market price of a good rises, the amount that existing producers are willing and able to supply will expand, and suggests that new producers might in addition be attracted into the market. Similarly, if the price falls, then the amount that existing producers are willing and able to supply will contract, and the least efficient producers might leave the market. Other conditions which will affect supply include the costs of **production**, the state of technology, the prices of other

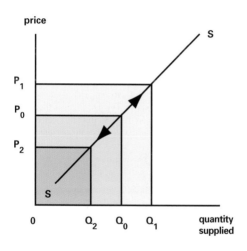

***supply*** *A price rise from $P_0$ to $P_1$ will cause an expansion in supply from $Q_0$ to $Q_1$. A price fall from $P_0$ to $P_2$ will cause a contraction in supply from $Q_0$ to $Q_2$.*

goods and services, and the level of **indirect tax** and **subsidies**.

## Supply of Goods and Services Act (1982)
*See* **Sale and Supply of Goods Act (1994)**.

**survey**   A method of **field research** carried out to establish the opinions and attitudes of individuals. In business, the most common type of survey is a **market research** survey where the attitudes of **consumers** to a product are being tested. Surveys may also be carried out amongst suppliers and retail outlets, and increasingly the opinions and ideas of employees are being sought through workforce surveys. Surveys may be carried out by postal questionnaire, by interview based on a questionnaire, by bringing together a panel or group of consumers, or by telephone. Many businesses use professional market research agencies to carry out their surveys. With any survey, it is important to ensure that the group of people who are surveyed form a representative sample of the whole population at which the survey is aimed.

# T

**take-home pay**   *See* **net pay**.

**takeover**   A situation where one company takes control over another company by persuading the **shareholders** of the second company to sell their shares to the first. This is usually done by offering the shareholders a better price for their shares than they might expect to achieve if they held onto their shares with the existing **management**. Takeovers in the UK may be referred to the **Monopolies and Mergers Commission** if the takeover would lead to a **market share** of more than 25% in the UK market by the new company, or if the value of the **assets** being transferred is greater than £5m. Directors of companies which are threatened by takeover often try to persuade their shareholders not to sell, or may invite a rival bid from a 'friendlier' competitor to prevent the original takeover. *See also* **merger**.

**tariff or custom duty**   A **tax** imposed by a government on the price of goods being imported into the country (*see* **customs and excise duties**). The tax might be charged as a certain percentage of the goods' value, or as an amount per unit. In less-developed countries, tariffs are a useful way for the government to raise revenue, but in developed countries their main purpose is to reduce the overall levels of **imports** in a country and to protect domestic industries from **competition** from overseas. Thus, a new industry or a declining industry may be given protection from cheaper imported goods to give the domestic producers a chance to establish themselves. Within the **European Union** there are no **tariffs** between the member states, but there is a common external tariff against outside countries. Governments throughout the world have generally tried to reduce the level of tariffs internationally through the General Agreement on Tariffs and Trade, in order to encourage and increase the level of world trade. *See also* **quota**.

**taxation**    The compulsory contribution of money to the government. It is the major source of income for governments. Taxation is used to finance government expenditure. It represents a transfer of income from individuals, groups and organizations to the government. Types of taxation are shown in the figures.

Direct taxation in the UK is *progressive* in that people with higher incomes will pay proportionately more in tax than people with low incomes. This helps to ensure that some income is redistributed from the well-off to the less well off. **Indirect taxes** tend to be *regressive,* in that the less welloff will be paying the same amount as the richer groups; this sum will represent a larger part of the income of the poorer

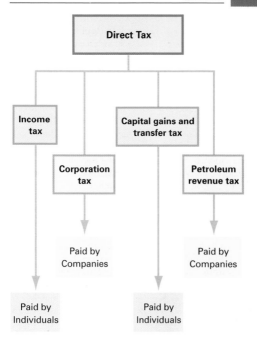

***taxation***
*(a) Direct taxes on wealth and income.*

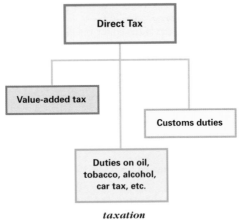

***taxation***
*(b) Indirect taxes on prices.*

group than the richer group. With **corporation tax,** all companies over a certain size pay the same percentage of their profits – this then is a proportional tax – but smaller firms pay a lower percentage or no tax, which provides a progressive element.

**Taylor, F.W. (1865–1915)**   The American founder of the school of scientific management, who was the first person to study work in a methodical and scientific way, while he was chief engineer at the Bethlehem Street

Company in the USA. He stressed the importance of looking at each element of a work task, timing it, seeking ways of improving the way that task was completed, and devising a system of financial awards which would motivate those completing a task. His approaches became popular with **management** because they could see possible gains in efficiency, but they became unpopular with the unions and the workforce because the workers seemed to be regarded as an 'inefficient' machine, and the methods employed could also make the work more monotonous and repetitive. *See also* **McGregor**, **Mayo**.

**TECs** *See* **Training and Enterprise Councils**.

**technology** The application of scientific discoveries and developments to the solving of problems. It is often applied to the production of **goods** and **services**. Technology allows the development of new goods and services, for example the microcomputer, digital watches, and computer cash dispensers outside banks. It also changes the way that existing goods and services are made and provided, for example automated **production lines**, battery farming and fast-food restaurants. Technology can benefit businesses and lead to greater efficiency and output and a better working environment, but it can also result in fewer jobs, less variety and craftsmanship in products, and a less responsible organization. The type of technology employed by a business has been found to have a considerable influence on the type of organization and communications within a business.

**tertiary production**   The provision of services which help to support the other two sectors of **business activity**, the primary and secondary. The tertiary sector includes professional services, administration, transport and **distribution**, financial services, and the public services, including health and education. This sector has grown in importance in terms of both **output** and employment within developed economies, as the secondary sector has declined. Although not regarded as 'wealth-creating', the tertiary sector generates an important part of domestic production, and through **exports** helps to increase earnings from overseas. Businesses in the tertiary sector tend to be more **labour-intensive** than the other two sectors, although development in **information technology** has brought a considerable number of computer applications into this sector and created many new services.

**test market**   A trial launch of a new product within a limited geographical area as part of the development of the product, especially in the **consumer goods** industry. This test market will allow the producer to carry out further **market research** about the product, and by judging its sales in the test area, to see if it will be successful on a nationwide basis. The area chosen within the UK may well correspond to a region of Independent Television, to allow for TV advertising, and the **consumers** in the area should have similar attributes to consumers nationally. A considerable number of products that are test-marketed do not go on to a national launch.

**time rate**  A **payments system**, in which employees are paid a set rate per hour or per week. The level of pay is therefore determined by the number of hours worked, irrespective of how much work is completed (*see* **piece rate**). For example, in a hotel a cleaner may be paid £4.75 per hour and work for four hours per day. In a five-day week, the **gross pay** will be £95.00 per week. The majority of employees are paid on a time rate system, with the possibility of them being paid an **overtime** rate for working extra hours. Although time rate does not provide an incentive to produce more goods, it is preferred by employee representatives because workers receive a basic wage irrespective of what stoppages or breakdowns have occurred in the workplace.

**Trade and Industry, Department of (DTI)**  A large UK government department which has overall responsibility for monitoring and encouraging the development of the industrial and commercial sectors of the economy. It is responsible for the operation of the **Office of Fair Trading**, and therefore oversees **consumer**

affairs, **restrictive practices**, **monopolies** and **mergers** and financial dealings. It is the channel for the government's provision of finance for industry; through its regional policy, providing grants for businesses starting up in areas of high **unemployment**, through direct investment in specific industries, and through grants to small business enterprises. It also aims to help and encourage UK companies in their export business by providing credit guarantees and advice and assistance with overseas markets. The DTI is run by a Secretary of State who is a member of the cabinet.

**trade credit**    A system of **credit** in which the supplier of a **good** to a business allows that business a period of time before it has to pay for the goods that it has received. The usual period is 30 days, and this can act as an important source of short-term finance for a business. It might be that the business is able to sell its finished goods before having to pay off the trade credit, thus avoiding the need to borrow further money from the bank. The level of trade credit owned by a business appears as a **liability** (*see* **current liabilities**) on its **balance sheet**. If the **creditor** wishes to receive the cash before the debt is due, then the debt may be sold to another agency at a **discount**, which will collect the money when it is due. This is known as *factoring* a debt. It is often common practice within the industry for trade credit to be given, especially to larger customers.

**Trade Descriptions Act (1972)**  A UK Act that ensures that **consumers** are not misled by the way **goods** and **services** are described in labels and in advertisements. Manufacturers, retailers and **advertising agencies** are held responsible for making sure that any description is true. The Act also covers the pricing of goods and services, and states that any notice which shows a reduced price or a cut in price must be genuine in that the goods must have been offered at a higher price within the last six months; while the prices for services such as a hotel meal must always be displayed. In advertising, although it is illegal to print something that is untrue, it is more difficult to decide when a description is just exaggerated as a sales technique rather than untrue. Other voluntary controls also exist over advertising. *See* **Advertising Standards Authority**.

**trade union**  A body representing a group of employees joined together as a single unit in order to represent their views and claims in negotiation with their employers. About 50% of the working population of the UK are members of trade unions. Three types of trade unions have developed, **craft**, **general** and **white-collar**, representing different types of worker, although in the 1980s there was an increase in the mixing of these types as a number of large **mergers** took place. A trade union will be administered by full time officials, and be under the control of a general secretary. Many are also affiliated to the **Trades Union Congress**.

**Trade Union Act (1984)**   A UK Act which brought in some legal controls over how **trade unions** operate. Elections for the senior officers in a trade union have now to be carried out by secret ballot, and a similar secret ballot has to be held before a decision is made to take **industrial action**. Trade unions are also required to hold a ballot to confirm that its members wish to make donations to political parties. Trade union activity was considerably affected in the 1980s by the **Employment Acts**, especially in relation to industrial disputes.

**Trade Union and Labour Relations (Consolidation) Act (1992)**   Act consolidating all earlier legislation on labour law, including the **Employment Acts**. It was amended in 1995 to bring it into line with EC requirements for union or employee representation in cases of redundancy or dismissal.

**trademark**   A particular **logo** which a business uses to distinguish its product from another one. Such a logo is registered to prevent others from copying it. For example, the Coca-Cola trademark is known throughout the world and represents an important **asset** for the company. The trademark will appear on the labels of the product, and also in any advertising or promotion connected to the product. It is therefore an important element in the **marketing** of a product.

**Trades Union Congress (TUC)**     Body founded in 1868 that is the nationwide representative organization for **trade unions** in the UK. Its role is to influence the government and other bodies to adopt policies favourable to trade unions, to develop a good image for trade unions, and to provide trade unions with research and publicity. Its annual congress is the main policy-making body, but there is also a full-time secretariat and a general council under a general secretary, which provide the leadership for the TUC. The TUC's main interests are in economic policy, employment policy and social policies, and it also represents British trade unions in international discussions. It is also involved in training and education for trade unionists, as well as in **industrial relations** through its involvement with **ACAS** and through acting as a mediator in disputes between unions.

**trading account**     The first part of a **profit-and-loss account** showing the **costs** and **sales revenue** resulting from the business's day-to-day trading activity and calculating the **gross profit** or gross loss. For a manufacturing company, the trading account could be made up of the items shown in the example overleaf. The closing stock of goods is deducted in the example overleaf, because these goods have not yet been sold during this period.

|  | £ | £ |
|---|---|---|
| **Sales revenue** |  | 25,000 |
| **LESS** |  |  |
| **Cost of goods sold** | 2,000 |  |
| **Opening stock** | 5,000 |  |
| **ADD** |  |  |
| **Purchases** | 5,000 |  |
|  | 23,000 |  |
| **LESS** |  |  |
| **Closing stock** | 5,000 |  |
| **Cost of goods sold** |  | 5,000 |
| **Trading profit** |  | 13,000 |

*trading account*

**Trading Standards Officers**   Officials who work for local government within a Trading Standards Department, whose job it is to investigate complaints made by **consumers** against businesses. These might involve any aspect of business behaviour that is covered by the various pieces of consumer legislation. This includes misleading descriptions, misleading prices, inaccurate weights and measures and unsafe products.

As well as carrying out inspections and investigations, these officers will pursue cases against traders into the courts to prevent further problems. They also provide advice and information for the public on consumer matters. *See also* **Consumer Safety Act**.

**training**   The process of improving and extending a person's skills or knowledge. An organization, or educational establishment on behalf of an organization, may provide an opportunity for an employee to acquire new knowledge and skills relating to his or her job and workplace. Such training might be **on-the-job** or **off-the-job**, or involve a combination of both. For the organization, the objectives of such training would be to develop a better informed and skilled workforce in order to improve the performance of the organization. For the individuals, training might help also to secure promotion or a new job, as well as helping him or her to do their job better. Training at the beginning of a job is known as **induction**, but increasingly employers are offering their workforce opportunities for training throughout their working life. Workers might also be offered the chance to retrain in a new set of skills, if their existing skills or experience are no longer relevant or needed.

## Training and Enterprise Councils (TECs)
Independent companies which have been set up by local employers, with local government representatives, and which aim to promote training on behalf of the

**Department for Education and Employment (DfEE).** TECs provide vocational training for young people in the form of *modern apprenticeships* and **Choices Training**. They also help people to start their own businesses and provide some training for older people.

**Treasury** This is the government department that is responsible for overseeing and carrying out the country's economic policies, including its fiscal and monetary policies. Under the Chancellor of the Exchequer, it is in charge of government expenditure, and through the Inland Revenue, the collection of taxes. It controls the **Bank of England** and through that the **money supply** and the external value of the currency. Although the Treasury is run by civil servants, its policies are directed by the government of the day.

**TUC** *See* **Trades Union Congress**.

**turnover** **1.** (*sales turnover*) The value of sales over a period of time (**sales revenue**). The **debtor** turnover ratio is used to calculate the debt collection period.
**2.** The rate at which a business sells its products, (the *rate of stock turnover*).
**3.** (*labour turnover*) The rate at which workers leave a business each year.

# U

**unemployment** The state of being without work. A situation where someone who is actively seeking work, but is unable to obtain work is described as *involuntary unemployment.* *Voluntary unemployment* is a situation where someone prefers to seek leisure rather than to work. Only a small part of unemployment is thought to be voluntary. Involuntary unemployment might be due to a number of reasons, as shown in the diagram on page 230.

A major objective of government policy in the UK since World War II has been to achieve full employment, although governments have differed in the way that they have pursued this objective. Businesses face the dilemma that increased automation might lead to increased unemployment of the workforce but increased profitability for their **shareholders**.

**unfair dismissal** The ending of a person's employment by an employer without good reason.

As a result of the **Employment Acts**, since 1972 employees have been protected against unfair dismissal; that is, a business must now have a fair reason to sack somebody, and must have gone about the **dismissal** in a reasonable way. Good reasons for a dismissal might be that the employee is incapable of doing the job or has been dishonest or dangerous in what they have done; or

| Cyclical Unemployment | due to a recession in the economy or in an industry |
| Frictional Unemployment | as the workforce moves from one job to another, or from one area to another |
| Seasonal Unemployment | in some industries, especially agriculture and tourism, the level of employment increases and decreases at particular times of the year |
| Structural Unemployment | where an industry or region has declined on a long-term basis, with those people made unemployed unable to find alternative work |

***unemployment***
*The types of involuntary unemployment.*

that the job no longer exists (**redundancy**). But if an employee feels that he or she has been unfairly dismissed, or that chances to improve performance have not been given, then he or she may pursue the case with the union representative, and ultimately with an **industrial tribunal** who will decide if the dismissal was fair.

**union representative**    A person who carries out a similar role to that of a **shop steward** in representing a group of **trade union** members in a place of work, but whereas shop stewards are normally found in manual occupations, union representatives are the equivalent in white-collar jobs. They play an important part in providing information and support for their members, collecting dues and passing on grievances to management, but are less involved in direct pay bargaining than shop stewards because of the different nature of pay bargaining in white-collar occupations.

**unit cost**    *See* **average cost**.

**unlimited liability**    A form of **liability** in which the owners of a business are personally responsible for all the losses of the business, irrespective of the amount of **capital** they have invested in it. This will be true for a **sole trader** and in the majority of **partnerships**. Thus if two people form a partnership, then both might have to meet all the liabilities of the business if it fails, even though they might have brought differing amounts of capital into the business. The owners might have to sell their personal property to finance losses. As a business grows in size, so **limited liability** becomes necessary, or else individual investors would not risk putting capital into a company if they might be liable for all that company's debts.

**unofficial strike**    An **industrial action** taken by a group of employees that has not been agreed to by a **trade union** or group of unions. Quite often such **strikes** are local in scale and last only a short time, although some gain in size and length and eventually are recognized by the union and therefore become **official strikes**. Those on unofficial strike do not receive any support or strike pay from the official union. In legal terms, however, there is no difference between unofficial and official strikes; both types now come under the changes introduced in the 1980s.

# V

**Value-Added Tax (VAT)**    The basic form of **indirect tax** which is used within the **European Union**. It is a tax charged at every point where **goods** or **services** are exchanged, from **primary production** to the final **consumer**. It is a tax on the difference between the sale price of the goods and services and the costs of the inputs that were used to make them, i.e. the value added at that stage of production. The tax is added on at each stage, but each trader can claim back the tax he/she has paid on the inputs, so that it is the final consumer who pays the whole tax. In the UK, the current rate of VAT is 17.5%, but some products, such as food and children's clothes, are zero-rated. From a business point of view, an increase in VAT, is likely to reduce the sales of products, as it will increase the price of a product, while a cut in VAT is likely to increase the sale of products.

**value analysis**    The process of ensuring that the quality of the product matches the price the customer is prepared to pay, thus giving value for money. Many customers are not prepared to pay the high price of a perfect product, because they only need a satisfactory one.

**variable costs**    Those **costs** which change directly with the **output** of a business. These are likely to include direct labour costs, overtime costs, raw material costs, fuel and power. As **output** expands, these costs will increase in proportion, although as a firm approaches full capacity the variable costs may start to increase at a faster rate than output as over-extending develops. *Compare* **fixed costs**.

**VAT**    *See* **Value-Added Tax**.

**venture capital**    A source of capital available to businesses where there is a certain amount of **risk** involved. Venture capitalists are companies that are willing to support risky projects, often in return for a seat on the **board of directors** or a significant shareholding.

**vertical merger**    The joining of two companies from different levels of **production** in a **merger**, to become one company. The oil industry is an example of a vertically integrated industry, with oil companies owning businesses at all three stages of production, as shown in the figure on the right.

For the business, the benefits of vertical integration are that supplies are assured and an immediate customer or outlet is available.

However, a business might not have expertise at operating at all three levels. For the **consumer**, such integration should allow more reliability in service, but the lack of **competition** at each level might lead to

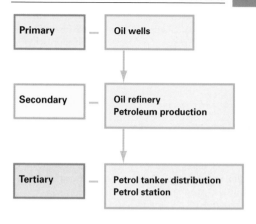

***vertical merger***
*An example of a vertically integrated company.*

higher prices. If a manufacturer takes over its supplier, the merger is known as *backward vertical integration*. If a manufacturer takes over its customer, the merger is known as *forward vertical integration*.

**Viewdata** The transmission of information via television screens to a large number of subscribers, for example, Oracle and Ceefax run by the IBA and the

BBC, and Prestel run by British Telecom. In such a system, data is provided by one set of organizations and is then called up onto a video screen by another set of organizations, with a charge being made for each page that is called up. It has proved most successful for organizations that are dealing with sets of data that need regular updating, such as stock market prices, exchange rates, or lists of TV programmes. Individuals may also be able to book services through Viewdata; it is used extensively in the travel industry for the booking of flights and holidays, and forms the basis for experiments in home banking and home shopping. However, the **Internet** has assumed many of the functions of Viewdata, and at a lower cost to businesses.

**visible trade**    This term is obsolete. It used to refer to the export and import of physical goods. Visibles are now referred to as **goods** in the **balance of payments**.

**voluntary codes of practice**    *See* **codes of practice**.

# W

**wage**   The basic reward paid for the provision of labour as a **factor of production**. A wage is usually paid on an hourly or weekly basis. Basic wages form an important element in **collective bargaining** between employees and management, and are regarded as one factor in motivating the workforce to increased output. Skilled workers who are in short supply are likely to be able to obtain higher wages than unskilled workers, or those workers in places where there are many people with similar skills. The different levels of wages that people receive are known as wage *differentials*. *See* **minimum wage**, **salary**, **motivation**.

**want**   The desire or need of a **consumer** to buy a **good** or **service**; if backed up by ability to pay, this becomes **demand**. *See also* **needs**.

**Weights and Measures Act (1985)**   A UK Act which contained elements of legislation going back to 1963 and earlier, and which covers aspects of control to protect **consumers**. **Trading Standards Officers** inspect regularly all equipment for weighing and measuring. **Goods** which are sold by weight or measure must be sold up to that weight or measure, i.e. traders should not give short weight or measure. Prepacked food must be marked with the weight or measure of its content, usually the net weight. It also established metric weights and measures as the UK standard.

**white-collar union**    A type of **trade union** which recruits workers in nonmanual occupations, including, for example, clerical workers, supervisors and administrators, professional, scientific and managerial staff, salespeople and shopworkers, artists and entertainers, and technicians. Membership of white-collar unions has grown along with the growth of **tertiary production**, especially in the **public sector** of the economy. Examples include NALGO, the local government officers' union, and NUT, a teachers' union. Growth of white-collar union membership in the private sector where many white-collar workers do not belong to a union, has been slow.

**wholesaler**    The middle person in a **channel of distribution** between producers and **consumers**, who plays the important role of breaking the bulk of what is produced by the manufacturers, and delivering the **goods** in smaller quantities to retailers. In the figure, the wholesaler helps to create an efficient **distribution** system from manufacturers to retailers; without the wholesaler there would need to be 18 separate links between manufacturers and retailers.

In some industries, however, either the manufacturer or the retailer has been taking on the function of wholesaling, thus cutting down the need to pay an

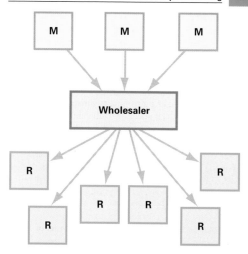

***wholesaler***
*The distribution system through the wholesaler from
manufacturers (M) to retailers (R).*

additional **mark-up** in price to the wholesaler. The major
costs incurred by wholesalers are transport and
warehousing ones.

**word processing** The storage and organization of
written text by electronic means. Many computer

programs have been written for creating and revising text that has been keyed into the computer's memory. Such programs are very flexible, allowing text to be corrected, moved around, amended, or added to, and allowing a **database** or graphics to be merged with text. Word processing is now extensively used in office and administrative work, and with increasingly sophisticated hardware and software, desk-top publishing is now possible on personal computers.

**work study**    A scientific study and analysis of work carried out by observers recording what work is done and how it is carried out. Such a study is carried out in order to find ways of increasing the **productivity** of a worker by improving the existing method of doing things, rather than by spending large sums of money on new machinery. The work being observed may be timed, and each element of the work described, and then the results are analysed to see if improvements could be made. Work study has been criticized for treating the workers as inefficient machines; it has been recognized that any work study should be carried out with the cooperation of those being studied, or else suspicion about possible changes and **redundancies** might occur in an organization.

**worker participation**    A situation where members of the workforce have some say in the decision-making of an organization. This might happen at various levels. At shop-floor level, it might involve regular meetings to discuss problems of a section of a firm, as in **quality circles**. At **management** level, the process might involve consultation and negotiation between management and employee representatives over decisions affecting the organization. At ownership level, it might involve the workers owning shares in the company as part of a **profit-sharing** scheme; or on rare occasions, the workforce owning the company through a workers' **cooperative** or workers' buy-out.

Greater worker participation has been encouraged in recent years to increase the **motivation** of the workforce in their involvement in and support for the objectives of the organization. Some EC regulations, such as the European Works Council Directive, mandate employee consultation procedures.

**working capital**    This represents the amount of short-term **capital** that a business has available to meet the day-to-day cash requirements of its operations. It is calculated by:

> **Current assets – Current liabilities**
> **= Working Capital**
> **(or Net Current Assets)**

The **current assets** of **stocks**, debtors and cash all form part of the working capital of a business, while the current liabilities of **trade creditors**, **overdraft** and expense **creditors** will all make demands on the working capital within a year. If a business increases the level of its operations, it will need to increase the level of its working capital or else it may face problems with its **cash flow**, which might then threaten the existence of the organization, irrespective of how profitable it is.

**working conditions**    A general term used to describe both the physical conditions under which a job takes place, e.g. heat, light, noise, etc., and the other non-monetary factors which are important in determining the way a job is done. These would include the number of people allocated to a task, the amount of time given to complete a task, the length of breaks allowed, the way the task is organized. It has been felt that these conditions are important in determining the **motivation** of the workforce and that improving working conditions will improve **productivity**, but it has also been recognized that factors outside the nature of the job and working conditions, e.g. social factors, involvement, responsibility and achievement, are also important. Governments have legislated to ensure that physical working conditions do not lead to health or safety problems for the workforce.

**working population**    Those people in a country's population who offer themselves for work. This would include employees in employment and in self-employment, as well as those who are registered unemployed. It will not include those below the school-leaving age or above retirement age, nor those within those ages who choose not to work, for example students at college, or those staying at home to look after children or the elderly. In 2001 in the UK, of a total population of some 59m, just over 28m made up the working population. Thus over one half of the population is supported by the other half.

**Working Time Regulations (1998)**   UK regulations implementing the European Working Time Directive. They limit the number of hours per week (on average) that a worker can be required to work to 48; although workers can choose to work additional hours, their employer cannot require them to do **overtime**. The regulations also establish: the right to one day off each week; an hour's rest if the working day is longer than six hours; 11 hours rest in each 24 hours; and four weeks' paid annual leave.

**work-to-rule**   A type of **industrial action**, where in pursuing a trade dispute, the members of a **trade union** make sure that in carrying out their duties they follow closely all the rules governing the job. Many of those rules might exist to cover problems which rarely occur, and so this will mean that the job takes much longer to complete. This effectively becomes a go-slow.
For the workforce, this means that they are disrupting **production** but not losing any wages in so doing. For **management** in some industries, this can have a major

effect on the production of **goods** or **services**, especially where safety is an important factor, as in the transport industry.

**written communication**    The basis of much **communication** in business. This includes letters, reports, memoranda, notices, email and telex messages. Although written communication is a slower form of communication than verbal or oral, it provides a record of what is being discussed so that disagreements are avoided and accuracy can be checked; it will also be more detailed than other forms of communication, with the possibility of technical points being explained and interpreted. Developments in **information technology** have allowed the production of written communication to be speeded up, while the accuracy and quality of presentation has been maintained; it has also allowed the development of new types of written communication, such as **electronic mail** and fax. *See also* **word processing**.

# Y

**Youth Training**   *See* **Choices Training**.